LIVELY PLAYS

for

YOUNG ACTORS

LIVELY PLAYS
for
YOUNG ACTORS

12 One-Act Comedies
for Stage Performance

by CHRISTINA HAMLETT

Publishers   Sterling Partners, Inc.   *Newton, MA*

Reprinted in 2005, 2008

Library of Congress Cataloging-in-Publication Data

Hamlett, Christina.
    Lively plays for young actors : 12 one-act comedies for stage performance / by Christina Hamlett.
    p. cm.
    Contents: The prince's dilemma -- The ghost of Hemstead House --Picture perfect -- Once upon a fairy tale -- Wedding bell blues -- Author! author! -- The magic mermaid -- Secret agents in disguise -- Where there's a will, there's a play -- Eat, drink, and be scary -- Mother Goose gumshoe -- It's an okie-dokie life.
    ISBN 0-8238-0308-2
    1. Children's plays, American. [1. Plays.] I. Title.
PS3558.A4446L58 1998
812'.54--DC21   98-14359
                                                      CIP
                                                      AC

Printed in Canada

Contents

LIVELY PLAYS

for

YOUNG ACTORS

The Prince's Dilemma

Characters

PRINCE ALI BABBA YABBA DABBA DOO
YASMINE
FORTUNETELLER
MARGARET
RODNEY ALEXANDER
CARLTON SMITHERS

TIME: *An afternoon in 1900.*
SETTING: *The court of* PRINCE ALI BABBA YABBA
DABBA DOO. *There are colorful satin floor pillows and
potted palms. Throne is center.*
AT RISE: PRINCE *is seated on throne, and is being enter-
tained with a dance by* YASMINE. *As she finishes and
bows to him for approval,* PRINCE *stifles a loud yawn.*
YASMINE (*Alarmed*): Does not my dance delight and en-
lighten you, Excellency?
PRINCE (*Shaking his head*): To the contrary. Had I been
awake to enjoy it, I'm sure I would have found it most
satisfactory.
YASMINE (*Approaching him*): How much did you miss?
PRINCE: Only a few minutes.
YASMINE (*Hands on hips*): It was only a few minutes *long*!

PRINCE: Well, perhaps you can do it again after the evening meal. (*Yawns again*)

YASMINE: My company *bores* you, Excellency?

PRINCE: Nothing of the sort. (*Explaining*) A night without rest has left me wanting sleep.

YASMINE: Are you haunted by an old dream, perhaps?

PRINCE (*Shaking his head*): Worse. Vexed by a talkative bride!

YASMINE (*Puzzled*): Do you *already* find fault with her, Excellency? She has been at the court but a brief time.

PRINCE (*Sighing*): Strange. It seems an eternity.

YASMINE: Yet her beauty bespeaks perfection.

PRINCE (*Somewhat annoyed*): Her mouth bespeaks non-stop chatter! She has—alas—fallen into a most annoying habit, Yasmine.

YASMINE (*Sitting on a pillow*): And what is that?

PRINCE: Every evening just before dusk she tells me a story.

YASMINE: But surely she seeks only to entertain and beguile you.

PRINCE: That's not the problem.

YASMINE: No?

PRINCE (*Indignantly*): She refuses to tell me the endings until dawn!

YASMINE (*Puzzled*): How very peculiar.

PRINCE: And how very annoying! I keep falling asleep! I have yet to hear how one comes out before she starts another!

YASMINE: Hm-m-m. How long has she practiced this strange and foreign custom?

PRINCE: It seems a thousand nights, at least. If she does it once more, I shall lose my sanity as readily as she shall lose her head!

YASMINE: Ah—but you outlawed beheadings just last month, Excellency. Have you forgotten?

PRINCE: Hm-m-m . . . so I did.

YASMINE: One must practice patience, my love.

PRINCE: Patience, indeed! It's one of the few virtues I am lacking.

YASMINE: True. You are still distressed by the prophecy of the gypsy girl, are you not, Excellency?

PRINCE: I'm distressed even more by the amount of silver with which I had to cross her palm. One should hear what one pays for.

YASMINE: Yet you paid to hear the future, however unpleasant . . . and that is what you received. (*Sighs*) You cannot take me as your 43rd bride until you have rid yourself by gift of wives number 41 and 42.

PRINCE: And as of this morning I'm only on wife 41—and who would take *her*?

YASMINE: But you must admit that she is beautiful. And perhaps her stories would beguile a stranger!

PRINCE: A *deaf* stranger, perhaps.

YASMINE: Perhaps.

PRINCE: That still doesn't solve the problem of number 42. Where will I meet her?

YASMINE (*Shrugging*): I don't know. Maybe someone will come to the door. (PRINCE *strokes his chin, pondering, then snaps his fingers.*) A plan of action, Excellency?

PRINCE: Yes! What I need to do is consult a reliable source.

YASMINE (*Putting hand to her ear*): Wait! I think I hear one coming now! (*A folded newspaper whizzes through the air and lands at* PRINCE's *feet;* YASMINE *picks it up, removes rubber band and unfolds paper.*)

PRINCE: What page?

YASMINE (*Scanning the listing*): D-17. (*Turns to appropriate page and holds it out for him*)

PRINCE (*Reading*): An active day for trading. The arrival of guests will mean costly repairs. An associate will assist you with decision-making. Get more rest.

YASMINE (*Taking the paper from him*): A favorable forecast, Excellency.

PRINCE (*Annoyed*): But no mention of matrimony.

YASMINE (*Indicating paper*): Still, it's only the early edition. Perhaps the evening news will print what you seek.

PRINCE (*Impatiently*): But I want to know now! (*Suddenly claps his hands three times loudly*)

YASMINE (*Surprised*): Is this belated applause for my dance, Excellency?

PRINCE: No. It's a summons to the palace fortuneteller.

YASMINE: An excellent idea!

PRINCE: Yes, isn't it?

FORTUNETELLER (*Entering and bowing to* PRINCE): Greetings and salutations, Excellency. I am here.

PRINCE: So you are. (*Folding his hands*) I would like a second opinion. You have been at my palace for the past seven years. You know all that will come to pass.

FORTUNETELLER (*Nodding*): More or less.

PRINCE: I want you to tell me what it is I want to know.

FORTUNETELLER: And what is that, Excellency?

PRINCE (*Puzzled*): What do you mean, "What is that?"

FORTUNETELLER: Exactly as it is phrased, Excellency.

PRINCE: But aren't you fortunetellers supposed to know these things by mind-reading?

FORTUNETELLER (*Patiently*): If it is an answer you seek, you must first ask the question.

PRINCE (*Exasperated*): I'll never understand how you people work!

FORTUNETELLER: You're not supposed to, Excellency. And now, what is your question?

PRINCE: What is my fate?

FORTUNETELLER: What is the date? (PRINCE *scratches his head, trying to remember.*)

YASMINE (*Helpfully*): The 21st.

FORTUNETELLER: Ah, yes, the 21st. (*Pauses*) And the date of your birth?

PRINCE: Is that important?

FORTUNETELLER: Crucial, Excellency.

PRINCE (*Scratching his head*): Hm-m-m. . . .

YASMINE: The ninth of next month.

FORTUNETELLER: Ah, yes. (*Stands silently for a moment*)

PRINCE: Well? What is in store for me?

FORTUNETELLER (*With eyes closed; concentrating*): I see . . . that it will be an active day for trading. The arrival of—hmm-m-m, this isn't quite clear, give me a moment. . . .

YASMINE: Guests, perhaps?

FORTUNETELLER: Yes, of course. Guests. Their arrival will mean costly repairs. And an associate—

PRINCE (*Annoyed, tossing the paper at* FORTUNE-TELLER's *feet*): We've read it already.

FORTUNETELER: Oh. (*Shrugging*) Then perhaps you'd like me to come back later when I've had more time to think about it.

PRINCE: You wouldn't want to lose your head, would you?

FORTUNETELLER (*Warning him*): I foresee disaster.

PRINCE: As clearly as unemployment? (FORTUNE-TELLER *closes eyes and concentrates; then, after a moment, begins talking.*)

FORTUNETELLER: I see the sands of the desert on which the winds of time have written the history of civilization. I see many camels. I see many men walking a mile for such a beast. I see footprints leading across the expanse of uninhabited land. . . . I see an oasis of green palms and merchants in stylish silk.

PRINCE (*Interrupting*): Do you perchance see this general neighborhood? This palace, perhaps?

FORTUNETELLER (*Continuing*): I hear the sound of gold

coin striking the palm (*Opens one eye to peer at* PRINCE) of those who are gifted to reveal the passages of future wisdom. (*Puts hands over ears*)

YASMINE: What's wrong?

FORTUNETELLER: The sound of coins is very loud. Can it be? Yes, it is. The vibrations are coming from this very chamber as someone who seeks knowledge from the beyond feels behooved to grant payment. (*Puts hand out to side, palm up;* PRINCE *reluctantly hands one gold coin to* YASMINE, *who places it in* FORTUNETELLER's *palm;* FORTUNETELLER *scowls.*) I hear angry gods conspiring and small birds cooing, "Cheap! Cheap!," throughout the walls of the palace. (PRINCE *gives* YASMINE *a few more coins.*) But, wait! I hear something else. A purse, perhaps . . . a purse heavy with gold coins. (PRINCE *pulls out velvet pouch, which* YASMINE *hands to* FORTUNE-TELLER.) I also foresee a two-week vacation in Cairo. (*Pauses*) One week in Cairo? (PRINCE *doesn't react.*) A weekend in Bombay, perhaps?

PRINCE (*Matter-of-factly*): The rest of the afternoon off.

FORTUNETELLER: Very well. The gods say you must marry the first foreigner who walks down the beach.

PRINCE: But we have a law against it!

FORTUNETELLER: Against walking on the beach?

YASMINE (*Shaking her head*): Against foreigners.

PRINCE (*Continuing*): They keep trying to bring us civilization.

YASMINE (*Lightly*): And goodness knows it's just a fad.

FORTUNETELLER (*Starting to exit*): You asked for a look at the future.

PRINCE: But it's not a future I want to have.

FORTUNETELLER: Would you incur the wrath of the gods by defying what they have chosen for you?

PRINCE: In a word, yes.

FORTUNETELLER: Then I must warn you of great doom.

YASMINE (*Curiously*): What kind of doom?

FORTUNETELLER (*Seriously*): Your rivers will run dry. . . . Your servants will mutiny one by one. The sky will rain elephants on your household. . . . The neighbors you once trusted will kick sand in your face and say, "nyeh, nyeh, nyeh."

YASMINE (*To* PRINCE): Sounds pretty serious to me.

FORTUNETELLER (*Nodding*): This it is. (*Exits*)

PRINCE: Drat! Where can I possibly find a foreigner walking along the beach? (*Suddenly a loud crunching and crashing noise is heard offstage.* PRINCE *looks off, alarmed.*) What was that?

YASMINE (*Pointing downstage as if out window*): Excellency! Look at that!

PRINCE (*Squinting*): Look at what?

YASMINE (*Pointing*): Out there. In the water. (PRINCE *scrambles to take glasses from pocket, puts them on.*) It's a ship! It ran into the dock. It's sinking!

PRINCE (*Exasperated*): Oh, terrific.

YASMINE: Excellency! Do you know what this means?

PRINCE (*Nodding*): It means my insurance rates are going to go up again.

YASMINE (*Grabbing his arm in excitement*): Survivors! Foreigners!

PRINCE: What?

YASMINE: Perhaps the ship will have survivors, and perhaps one of them will be a woman, and perhaps she'll say yes if you ask her to be your wife. (MARGARET *strides into room, hands on her hips. She stops, looks around.*)

MARGARET: All right. Who's in charge here?

YASMINE (*Taken aback*): And who are you?

MARGARET (*Matter-of-factly*): I'm a victim of circumstance and negligence.

PRINCE: Is that a name or a title?

MARGARET: It happens to be a state.

YASMINE (*Aside; to* PRINCE): It must be over in that New World they're always talking about.

MARGARET (*Continuing*): A state and condition for which I hold the builder of that structure out in the water totally responsible.

PRINCE: The structure you're referring to happens to be a dock.

MARGARET: Well, that dock just hit my ship.

YASMINE: Are you from the ship?

MARGARET: Of course. That's what I just said.

PRINCE: And you just now walked up the beach?

MARGARET: Of course I walked up the beach. I demand to be taken to someone in charge.

YASMINE (*With a sweep of her hand toward* PRINCE): Ta-da! May I introduce Prince Ali Babba Yabba Dabba Doo?

MARGARET: Now we're getting somewhere. How do you do?

PRINCE: Marvelously, thank you. Would you like to marry me?

MARGARET: I beg your pardon?

YASMINE: Provided, of course, that you're a foreigner.

PRINCE (*To* YASMINE): Of course she's a foreigner. She'll be just fine. (*To* MARGARET) You will say yes, won't you?

MARGARET (*Confused*): Say yes to what?

YASMINE: His proposal of matrimony.

PRINCE (*Eagerly*): Do you accept?

MARGARET: You don't even know my name or a thing about me!

PRINCE: Nonsense. I've had it foretold by tellers of fortunes. You're 42.

MARGARET (*Shocked*): They're way off. I'm not a day over 33. (*Suddenly, another loud crash is heard offstage.*)

PRINCE: What was that?

YASMINE (*Pointing as before*): Excellency! Look!

PRINCE: What is it?

YASMINE: Another ship.

PRINCE: Not the dock again?

MARGARET: (*Looking; in alarm*): Oh, no! How terrible!

YASMINE (*Consoling her*): No, it's all right. He was going to have it repaired anyway.

MARGARET: But that ship—it's his.

YASMINE: Whose?

MARGARET: The dreadful man I'm trying to get away from.

PRINCE: And who is he?

MARGARET: He's a cad and a fortune hunter and a thoroughly disgusting individual.

YASMINE: And how did you come to know him?

MARGARET: He's my fiancé. (*Explaining*) My parents picked him out, unaware of his checkered past and his designs on my inheritance. I sailed away to escape from him.

PRINCE: Perhaps he went down with the ship.

MARGARET (*Pointing*): Oh, no! Look at that!

PRINCE: What?

MARGARET: That man in the rowboat.

PRINCE (*Squinting*): What rowboat?

YASMINE (*To* PRINCE): The one that's headed this way.

MARGARET (*Looking around*): You'll have to hide me!

PRINCE: Why?

MARGARET: Because he's here to take me back, and I'll have to marry him and live wretchedly ever after!

YASMINE: But what if you were married to someone else first?

MARGARET: But whom could I marry? (YASMINE *points to* PRINCE.) Oh, yes, you did say something about marriage, didn't you?

PRINCE: Yes, I did.

MARGARET (*Looking anxiously out window, then back to* PRINCE): How soon can we have the ceremony performed?

PRINCE (*Taking ring off his finger and sliding it onto one of* MARGARET's): Done!

MARGARET: Done?

PRINCE: We're now married. It's all quite legal. (*Indicating* YASMINE) We even have a witness.

YASMINE (*Dabbing her eyes*): How lovely. I always cry at weddings.

MARGARET (*To* PRINCE): Now, what did you say your name was?

RODNEY (*Striding into room; confidently*): Margaret! There you are!

MARGARET (*To* RODNEY): What are you doing here?

RODNEY (*Crossing and taking her wrist*): Bringing you to your senses.

MARGARET (*Shaking him off*): My senses are quite fine, thank you. Why don't you run along?

RODNEY: Run along in what? My ship just ran aground!

MARGARET: Yes, and I'm terribly sorry to hear that. (*Linking her arm through* PRINCE's) Maybe if you ask politely, my husband will build you a new one so you can get home.

RODNEY: Your husband?

MARGARET: Oh, excuse me—I've forgotten to introduce you, haven't I? Rodney Alexander, I'd like you to meet. . . . (*Hesitates*) my husband.

PRINCE (*Introducing himself*): Prince Ali Babba Yabba Dabba Doo.

RODNEY: Oh, yeah?

MARGARET: We would have invited you to the wedding, but we wanted to keep it small.

RODNEY: You're trying to tell me here that you're—uh— Mrs. Ali Babba—(*Pauses trying to remember the rest of it*)

YASMINE: Yabba Dabba Doo.

RODNEY (*To* YASMINE): Thanks. (*To* MARGARET) Is that what you're trying to say, Margaret?

MARGARET: Yes. I'm going to have it printed on my stationery next week.

RODNEY: Are you really married to this guy?

MARGARET: Yes. (*Indicating* YASMINE) We even had a witness.

YASMINE (*Nodding*): It was so lovely, I cried.

RODNEY (*To* PRINCE): But you don't know the first thing about Margaret.

PRINCE: There's only one thing that's important, as far as I'm concerned.

RODNEY: And what's that?

PRINCE: She's 42.

RODNEY: Forty-two? Ha! She's not a day over 33. (*Loud crash offstage is heard.*)

PRINCE (*Confused*): Where have I heard all this before?

YASMINE: It must be *déjà vu.*

MARGARET (*Looking out window*): No, it isn't. Look—it's another shipwreck.

PRINCE: Another one!

YASMINE (*Sighing*): This just doesn't seem to be your day, Excellency.

MARGARET (*Happily*): Oh, my! How wonderful!

RODNEY: What's wonderful?

MARGARET: The man coming this way in a rowboat. It's Carlton. The man I want to marry.

RODNEY (*Scowling; to* MARGARET): May I remind you of something?

MARGARET: What is it?

RODNEY (*Indicating* PRINCE): What are you going to do about him? Your husband—remember?

MARGARET (*Shrugging*): Oh, well, that's simple enough.

(*Removes ring and hands it to* PRINCE) It's been wonderful, of course, but the time has come to say goodbye. I hope we can still be friends. (*Turns and rushes into* CARLTON's *arms as he enters*) Carlton!

CARLTON (*Embracing her*): Margaret! How lovely you look. Is that a new dress?

RODNEY: Good grief!

CARLTON (*To* RODNEY; *annoyed*): What are you doing here?

RODNEY: I came here to collect my bride.

CARLTON (*Putting his arm around* MARGARET): I'm afraid you're too late. (*To* MARGARET) Isn't that so, dearest?

RODNEY (*To* MARGARET): What about the prince?

MARGARET: Oh, yes! Carlton, I'd like you to meet a dear friend. Ah-h . . . (*She can't remember* PRINCE's *name, so she proceeds to introduce* CARLTON.) And this is Carlton Smithers.

RODNEY: She still hasn't explained, Smithers, that you and I are both out of the running.

CARLTON: What do you mean?

PRINCE (*Interrupting*): She can't marry you—she's already married to me.

CARLTON: And who are you?

MARGARET: Have you forgotten already? I just introduced you.

CARLTON (*Dramatically*): Margaret, tell me it's not true.

MARGARET: It's not true.

RODNEY: She's lying.

MARGARET: Nonsense. (*To* PRINCE) I just gave you your ring back.

PRINCE: But it doesn't work that way.

MARGARET: It was easy enough getting married. Why are you being so difficult?

CARLTON: Do you mean that you're actually married to this person, Margaret? (*Shaking his head*) I'm really disappointed.

MARGARET: Carlton. . .

CARLTON: You've toyed with my affections, Margaret. I'm not entirely sure that I can find it in my heart to forgive you.

RODNEY: Way to go, Smithers!

MARGARET (*To* RODNEY): Oh, quiet down, Rodney. (*To* PRINCE) It's all your fault.

PRINCE: I'm sorry, but rules are rules.

YASMINE (*Suddenly*): Excellency!

PRINCE: Yes?

YASMINE: What if you were to obey the prophecy?

PRINCE: Which part?

YASMINE: Bestow a gift upon a willing receiver.

PRINCE: Hmm . . . they both seem willing enough . . . .

YASMINE: May I make a suggestion?

PRINCE: Certainly. (*She whispers in his ear. He ponders a moment, then addresses* CARLTON.) Oh, Smithers? Was that your name?

CARLTON: Carlton Smithers, yes.

PRINCE: Since you are clearly the worthier of receivers to take the gifts of Margaret's charm and company, I therefore give her to you.

MARGARET (*Indignantly*): What do you mean, you *give* me to him? What am I—excess baggage?

CARLTON: Your offer, though most generous, sir, is quite uncalled for.

PRINCE: And how so?

CARLTON: Because Margaret is a woman of the world, not a common possession to be bought, sold, or traded. She is ahead of her time, a lady of impeccable taste, charm, wisdom and creativity, not to mention a will of steel and a mind of her own. I cannot permit you to treat her as less.

PRINCE (*Shrugging*): You can take her, or I can have her be-
headed.

MARGARET (*Throwing herself at* CARLTON): Take me!
I'm yours!

RODNEY: What about me?

PRINCE: What about you?

RODNEY: You have dared to label me unworthy, and yet I
am destined for fame and fortune.

YASMINE: Fame and fortune? How curious! And what do
you do?

RODNEY: I am a writer.

MARGARET (*Laughing*): Writer? Ha!

PRINCE: It would seem that your work is not taken seriously in this company.

CARLTON: Cheap thrillers and tawdry romance can hardly
be deemed a claim to reward and recognition.

MARGARET: That's why he wanted to marry me, so that
my family could support his questionable vocation.

RODNEY: So, I've had a dry spell lately. It can happen to
anyone.

CARLTON: So dry, there's *dust* on it!

RODNEY: For your information, the book I'm working on
promises to be most sensational.

MARGARET: A title alone does not a novel make.

RODNEY: It takes time to build momentum.

YASMINE: And what's the title?

RODNEY: *A Collection of Astounding Adventures of the
Bold and Chivalrous Noblemen and Soldiers of Arabia.*

PRINCE: That's rather long, isn't it?

YASMINE: Why don't you call it *The Arabian Knights*?

RODNEY: Hmm-m-m. Not bad. It might have possibilities.

PRINCE: What's it about?

RODNEY (*Awkwardly*): I'm not quite sure yet.

PRINCE: What do you mean?

RODNEY: My flights of fantasy keep escaping. Many a sleepless night I've pondered on a possible plot, yet none of enduring substance have intrigued me.

PRINCE (*Intrigued*): Sleepless nights?

RODNEY: I'm often awake until dawn, lying in wait for inspiration.

YASMINE: Excellency!

PRINCE: Yes? (*She whispers in his ear; he smiles, then turns to* RODNEY.) There is a gift I wish to give you before you take leave of us.

RODNEY: A gift? And what sort?

PRINCE: A collaborator—my beautiful 41st wife—to assist with your notable endeavor.

RODNEY (*Intrigued*): I'm all ears.

PRINCE: Good. Your ears will be put to good use. My wife is quite a storyteller.

YASMINE: And now we can be married, Excellency.

PRINCE: Yes, Yasmine. Would you honor us with a dance of celebration?

YASMINE (*Smiling*): With pleasure. (YASMINE *begins to dance as others watch. Curtain slowly closes.*)

THE END

PRODUCTION NOTES

THE PRINCE'S DILEMMA

Characters: 2 female; 4 male.

Playing Time: 25 minutes.

Costumes: Margaret, Rodney and Carlton wear turn-of-the-century dress. Prince wears long, flowing robes, turban, several rings, and has bag of gold coins and eyeglasses in pocket. Fortuneteller may wear elaborate robe. Yasmine has brightly-colored pantaloons, loose blouse, and bright scarves around her head.

Properties: Folded newspaper.

Setting: The court of Prince Ali Babba Yabba Dabba Doo. There are colorful satin floor pillows and potted palms. Throne is center.

Sound: Loud crashes as ships hit dock.

The Ghost of Hemstead House

Characters

CLARENCE CLARIBONE, *young farmer*
SHERIFF LUDLOWE, *defender of law and order*
PRUNELLA BITTERSNAP, *librarian*
JASPER JOHANNSON, *bookkeeper*
JUDITH WITHERSPOON, *schoolteacher*
MAX A. MILLION, *stranger in town*

TIME: *Saturday morning, the present.*
SETTING: *Sheriff Ludlowe's cluttered office in Hemstead Crossing, a rural town. A desk at right is overflowing with papers, newspapers, a telephone, and Sheriff's morning snack and thermos. Up center is window looking out on a typical small-town street. Exit is stage left. Two chairs are left of desk and two other chairs are by window.*
AT RISE: SHERIFF LUDLOWE *sits at desk, reading paper and drinking coffee. Suddenly door bursts open and* CLARENCE CLARIBONE *runs into the room.*
CLARENCE (*Loudly*): Sheriff! Sheriff! (SHERIFF, *startled, jumps and his paper flies into air.*)
SHERIFF: Good grief, Clarence! You're always barging in.

What's all the ruckus about? You look as if you just shook hands with a ghost.

CLARENCE (*Anxiously looking behind him, then confidentially leaning over desk*): Too close for comfort, if you ask me, Sheriff!

SHERIFF (*Puzzled*): What's too close for comfort?

CLARENCE: *Ghosts.*

SHERIFF (*Confused*): Ghosts? (*Pauses*) Do you feel O.K., Clarence?

CLARENCE: Fit as a fiddle, Sheriff!

SHERIFF (*Shaking his head*): You must have a couple of strings out of kilter if you're seeing ghosts, Clarence.

CLARENCE: I didn't actually *see* one. (*Insisting*) But I know it was there!

SHERIFF: Where?

CLARENCE (*Pointing left*): Up at the old Hemstead house!

SHERIFF (*Laughing*): Come on, Clarence. Nothing's happened up at Hemstead house for a good thirty years! (*Picks up newspaper to resume reading*)

CLARENCE: Well, it's happening now, Sheriff. (*Shakes head*) No mistake—she's up there.

SHERIFF: Who?

CLARENCE (*Exasperated*): The ghost.

SHERIFF (*Skeptically*): How do you know it's a ghost, Clarence?

CLARENCE (*Pulling pink scarf from pocket and displaying it to* SHERIFF): Because she left this.

SHERIFF (*Looking at scarf*): Very pretty. Whoever lost this will be glad to get it back. Just drop it in the Lost and Found box. (*Continues reading*)

CLARENCE (*Pulling down paper to regain* SHERIFF's *attention*): But it's hers, Sheriff! It belongs to the ghost!

SHERIFF (*Shaking head*): There's no such thing, Clarence. It's all in your imagination.

CLARENCE: Sheriff, don't you think you ought to take a run up to the house and check it out?

SHERIFF (*Nervously*): Well, gee, Clarence, I'm pretty busy right now. (*Rearranges papers on desk*) Why don't *you* go up there? If you find any ghosts, let me know.

CLARENCE (*Cautiously backing up*): You won't catch me up there, Sheriff! That place gives me the creeps. (*Door behind him quietly opens and* PRUNELLA BIT-TERSNAP *enters, clutching three or four books.* CLAR-ENCE *doesn't hear her as he is backing up.*) You always get this feeling someone's going to sneak up behind you. . . . (PRUNELLA *reaches out and taps* CLAR-ENCE *on the shoulder; he shrieks.*)

PRUNELLA (*With her finger to her lips*): Shhhhh!

SHERIFF (*Rising from his chair*): Good morning, Miss Bittersnap. (*Pleasantly*) How are things at the library?

PRUNELLA (*Striding toward him; in annoyed tone*): Sheriff, I have a complaint.

SHERIFF: What about?

PRUNELLA (*Matter-of-factly*): About the noise that woke me up last night. (*Firmly*) I want it stopped immediately.

SHERIFF (*Scratching his head*): Miss Bittersnap, I can't stop it if I don't know what it is.

PRUNELLA (*Disgustedly*): Music. It woke me up, and I couldn't get back to sleep. Why, I couldn't even read, it was such a racket!

SHERIFF: What kind of music was it?

PRUNELLA: *Loud* music.

CLARENCE: It must be those Claridge boys and their rock group.

SHERIFF: I'll tell them to keep it down, Miss Bittersnap.

PRUNELLA (*Correcting him*): It's not them.

CLARENCE: Then who is it?

PRUNELLA: A woman. She kept singing the same song all

night. I couldn't concentrate on my reading, she was singing so loud.

SHERIFF: What time did all of this start?

PRUNELLA (*Shaking head*): I can't seem to recall. But I
can tell you one thing. (*Mysteriously*) I'm sure it was coming from the old Hemstead house. (CLARENCE *gasps;*
PRUNELLA *turns to him, her finger to her lips.*) Shhhh!

SHERIFF: That's pretty peculiar.

PRUNELLA (*Distressed*): Don't you believe me?

SHERIFF (*Looking at her*): A voice would have to be pretty
loud to carry that far, Miss Bittersnap. (*Pauses*) Are you
sure it wasn't a car radio, or maybe the TV turned up loud?

PRUNELLA (*Emphatically*): Positive. It was a woman at
the Hemstead house.

CLARENCE (*Skeptically*): I wouldn't bet on it.

PRUNELLA: What are you talking about?

SHERIFF: Clarence has this foolish notion about seeing a
ghost.

CLARENCE: I didn't say I saw it. What I said was that she
left this. (*Holds up scarf*)

PRUNELLA (*Grabbing scarf*): Oh, my!

SHERIFF (*Concerned*): What is it, Miss Bittersnap?

PRUNELLA (*Slowly*): It looks like the one *she* wore!

SHERIFF *and* CLARENCE (*Together*): Who?

PRUNELLA: The ghost of Hemstead house.

CLARENCE (*To* SHERIFF): I told you!

PRUNELLA (*Continuing*): She always wears it. That's what
folks who've seen her say! (*Sits*)

SHERIFF: Have *you* ever seen her, Miss Bittersnap?

PRUNELLA: I haven't, but my mother saw her once. (*Shaking her head*) "It's a sight I'll remember all my days, Prunella." That's what she used to say to me.

CLARENCE: As I said, Sheriff, maybe you'd better run up
and take a look.

SHERIFF (*Sitting*): It would be a waste of time. There's no such thing as ghosts. (*There is a sudden sharp knock at the door.*)

CLARENCE (*Nervously*): What was that?

SHERIFF: Someone's at the door. (CLARENCE *doesn't move.*) For heaven's sake, Clarence—open the door. (CLARENCE *reluctantly crosses to door and opens it.*)

CLARENCE (*Turning to* SHERIFF): Uh . . . no one's there. (*As he turns to close door,* JASPER JOHANNSON *appears, holding a shovel, and startles* CLARENCE.) Ah-h!

PRUNELLA: Shhhh!

JASPER: Uh . . . sorry to scare you like that, Clarence.

SHERIFF: Good morning, Jasper.

JASPER (*Tipping his hat*): Morning, Sheriff—Miss Prunella. (*Reaches inside door and props shovel against wall*) I'll just leave this here and be on my way. (*Ducks out*)

SHERIFF (*Shouting*): Jasper!

JASPER (*Timidly reappearing*): Yes, Sheriff?

SHERIFF (*Indicating the shovel*): I suppose you've got an explanation for this?

JASPER (*Awkwardly*): Well, I found it on my way home from the bank last night. It was in the ground.

CLARENCE (*Nodding*): Good place for a shovel.

SHERIFF (*Insistently*): What ground, Jasper?

JASPER: Here in town.

SHERIFF: Any particular place?

JASPER (*Hesitating*): Well, gee—uh . . .

SHERIFF, PRUNELLA *and* CLARENCE (*Together; annoyed*): Where was the shovel, Jasper?

JASPER (*Quickly*): By the gate leading up to the Hemstead house!

CLARENCE (*To* SHERIFF): I told you!

SHERIFF: Do you have any idea what it was doing there, Jasper?

JASPER (*Shrugging*): At the time, it wasn't doing anything. It was just sitting there right where they dropped it.

PRUNELLA: Who?

JASPER: Whoever was doing the digging.

SHERIFF: What were they digging, Jasper?

JASPER (*Shaking his head*): I don't really know. It looked like a big hole.

PRUNELLA: Maybe they were planting nasturtiums.

CLARENCE (*Eerily*): Or a *body*.

JASPER (*Considering*): It could have been a body. The hole was big enough for a body.

SHERIFF: Did you see anybody suspicious hanging around?

JASPER: Everybody in this town looks suspicious. (JUDITH WITHERSPOON *enters, carrying a bouquet of flowers;* CLARENCE's *back is to her.*)

CLARENCE: As I said, Sheriff, the next thing you know they'll be walking into town in broad daylight and scaring the socks off us! (*Turns around and bumps into* JUDITH. *He shrieks again.*)

JUDITH (*Sweetly*): I'm sorry—did I frighten you, Mr. Claribone?

CLARENCE (*Bravely*): Of course not! Not at all! (*Admires her*) You're looking fine today, Miss Witherspoon.

JUDITH (*Worriedly*): I'm not so sure that I *feel* so fine.

PRUNELLA (*Concerned*): Is something wrong, Judith? (CLARENCE *and* JASPER *both rush to bring a chair center stage; she smiles at both of them and sits.*)

JUDITH: Well, it all started with these flowers.

PRUNELLA: They're lovely. Are they a present from your class?

JUDITH: Actually, the children *found* them.

SHERIFF: As long as they didn't pick them. (*Reminds her*) We've got an ordinance about robbing nature, you know.

JUDITH: Oh, they'd never do that, I know, but . . . .

JASPER: But what?

JUDITH: Well, they said they *found* them, but they were hesitant to tell me where.

PRUNELLA: Maybe they took them from someone's garden and thought they'd get in trouble.

JUDITH: No, it wasn't that. (*Pauses*) You see, they said they found them on the steps of the old Hemstead house!

SHERIFF (*Shaking head*): Those kids shouldn't be nosing around the Hemstead place.

JUDITH (*Placing flowers on desk*): Oh, I'm sure it was all an innocent prank, Sheriff. Ordinarily, I'd have thought nothing of it, but something up there at the house gave them the scare of a lifetime. They said they heard voices and saw shadows in the windows.

CLARENCE: I know how they feel.

JUDITH (*Puzzled*): I beg your pardon?

PRUNELLA (*To* SHERIFF): And don't forget that woman I heard singing!

JASPER (*Piping up*): Or the shovel down at the gate!

JUDITH: Will someone please tell me what's going on here?

JASPER, CLARENCE *and* PRUNELLA (*Ad lib*): Let me tell you all about it. Here's what happened. (*Etc. Suddenly, three very loud thumps on the door are heard; everyone stops talking to look toward door.*)

PRUNELLA (*Nervously clutching her books*): What was that?

JASPER: I think someone's at the door.

SHERIFF (*Firmly*): Open the door, Clarence.

CLARENCE (*Upset*): I opened the door last time! (*Points to* JASPER) Why doesn't he answer the door?

JASPER: Why me?

JUDITH (*Rising*): Never mind, I'll get it.

CLARENCE: I was just kidding. (*Goes to the door*) I'll get it.

JASPER (*Trying to head him off*): I'll get it. (*The two nearly collide with each other;* JUDITH *calmly walks to door and opens it to* MAX A. MILLION, *who wears long cape, jaunty beret, and dark glasses, and carries a brightly-colored megaphone.*)

MAX (*Surveying* JUDITH): Are you, by chance, the constable?

JUDITH (*Laughing*): No. (*Extends her hand*) I'm Judith Witherspoon.

MAX (*Shaking her hand*): Charmed, I'm sure. (*Anxiously*) I must find the constable immediately.

JUDITH (*Pointing to* SHERIFF): Search no further.

MAX (*Striding into room, extending hand to* SHERIFF): How do you do?

SHERIFF: Hello. I'm Sheriff Ludlowe. What can I do for you?

MAX: I want to report some missing property.

SHERIFF (*Rummaging through forms on his desk*): What kind of property is missing, Mr. —

MAX: Million. Max A. Million.

SHERIFF: What exactly are you missing, Mr. Million? (*Hands him forms and pen*)

MAX: Well, I'm missing—(*His glance falls on flowers.*) Aha! (*Holds up flowers, looks around at others*) Where did these come from?

JUDITH: My students brought them to me. (*Pauses*) Are they yours?

MAX (*Ignoring* JUDITH; *muttering to himself*): If I've told him once, I've told him a thousand times, not to leave things lying around. (*Sees shovel*) Aha! (*Runs over to it*)

SHERIFF: Is something wrong, Mr. Million?

MAX (*Pointing*): Where did you get that shovel?

JASPER: I found it last night, on the ground.

MAX (*Annoyed*): That Henry's going to set us back a good month if we have to keep buying new props!

PRUNELLA: Who's Henry?

MAX (*To* PRUNELLA): Henry Milksap, my assistant. (*Picks up shovel*) If he's not more careful, we'll *never* finish this picture!

ALL but MAX (*Together*): *What* picture?

MAX: I suppose I'll have to tell you all about it now, if I want to get my props back.

SHERIFF: I'm afraid so. (*Hands on hips*) Now, do you mind telling us what's going on?

MAX (*Matter-of-factly*): Not at all. We've been in town for two days filming a picture.

PRUNELLA (*Primping*): A *movie* picture? My goodness, what's it all about?

MAX: Do you know that old mansion up on the hill?

SHERIFF (*Nodding*): Hemstead house.

MAX: It seems that there's a legend about its being haunted—ever hear it?

SHERIFF (*Nodding wearily*): All morning.

MAX: Anyway, we thought it would make a great release for this summer. Big name stars, special effects . . .

PRUNELLA (*Suddenly; beginning to understand*): Any music?

MAX (*Nodding*): The ghost's theme song. Not very catchy, just eerie. (*Pauses*) The soprano must've done it a hundred times last night to get it right.

JASPER: What about the shovel?

JUDITH: And the flowers?

MAX: All props—(*Dramatically*) things we use to make the show really come alive!

SHERIFF: How come we didn't know anything about this? It's a pretty big deal, having movie people come out here.

MAX: That's exactly why we had to keep it secret, Sheriff. With too many people around, we couldn't wrap up the shooting on schedule.

PRUNELLA: Are you almost finished?

MAX (*Mulling it over*): All except for this short scene when the villagers are talking about the ghost.

JUDITH (*Eagerly*): How many villagers do you need?

MAX (*Innocently*): Oh, let me see. Three men and two women. Do you know anyone?

SHERIFF (*Gesturing toward others*): How about us?

MAX (*Doubtfully*): *You?*

JUDITH: Sure, why not? We could play the villagers as well as anyone else!

MAX (*Uncomfortably*): Well, gee, I don't know . . . (*Picks up megaphone and starts to leave*)

SHERIFF (*Quickly*): Then again, there is that new ordinance . . . .

MAX (*Turning*): What new ordinance?

SHERIFF: The one about shooting movies on location in Hemstead Crossing. (*Shakes head*) There's a whopper of a fine if you don't have a license.

JUDITH (*To MAX*): You do have a license, don't you?

MAX (*Pondering for a moment, then announcing*): How would you all like to be on the set tomorrow morning, five o'clock sharp?

ALL (*Ad lib; pleased*): Great! Sounds good! (*Etc.*)

MAX: Fine. Now, don't be late. (*Starts to exit*)

CLARENCE (*Running to MAX*): Oh, Mr. Million?

MAX (*Turning*): Yes?

CLARENCE: You almost forgot something.

MAX (*Puzzled*): I did?

CLARENCE (*Pulling out scarf*): This.

MAX (*Examining it*): It's very pretty. (*Hands it back to CLARENCE*)

CLARENCE (*Puzzled*): But, isn't it one of your props?

MAX: No, it isn't. In fact, I've never seen it before in my life. (*Exits, leaving the rest shocked, looking at each other in disbelief. Curtain*)

THE END

PRODUCTION NOTES

THE GHOST OF HEMSTEAD HOUSE

Characters: 4 male; 2 female.

Playing Time: 20 minutes.

Costumes: Modern dress. Sheriff Ludlowe wears sheriff's uniform, Max
A. Million wears a long cape, beret, and sunglasses.

Properties: Pink scarf, 3 or 4 books, shovel, bouquet of flowers, megaphone.

Setting: Sheriff Ludlowe's cluttered office in Hemstead Crossing. A desk at
right overflows with papers, newspapers, a telephone, Sheriff's morning
snack, thermos and mug. Up center is window looking out on typical
small-town street. Two chairs are left of desk, and two other chairs are
by window. Exit is stage left.

Sound: Knocks at door.

Picture Perfect

Characters

JULIAN GRAY, *wealthy art collector*
HOBBS, *Julian's butler*
MRS. BASS, *Julian's housekeeper*
MISS FINCH, *downstairs maid*
MISS APPLEGATE, *upstairs maid*
EDDIE
DARLA WHITE, *Julian's sweetheart*
CINDY, *Darla's friend*
BARTLETT

SCENE 1

TIME: *The present.*
SETTING: *Elegant drawing room of Julian Gray's house, filled with many sculptures; several paintings are hung on walls. Sofa, chair, and coffee table are center stage; needlepoint pillows are on both sofa and chair. Down right is a large potted plant and an umbrella stand. Upstage right is a closet with a working door. Upstage left are double doors leading into the room.*
AT RISE: JULIAN GRAY, *a dashing young man who is dressed for a formal occasion, bursts into the room, followed by HOBBS.*

JULIAN (*Upset*): You're absolutely certain you've looked everywhere?

HOBBS (*Emphatically*): Everywhere and twice over, sir. It's simply gone.

JULIAN: That's not good enough.

HOBBS: No, sir.

JULIAN: I want the house turned upside down.

HOBBS (*Sighing*): Very well, sir.

JULIAN (*As he crosses to sofa*): And when you're finished with it upside down, you can start all over from right side up.

HOBBS: As you wish, sir. (JULIAN *begins searching under the pillows.*) Begging your pardon, sir, but I've already looked there.

JULIAN (*Looking away, in dismay*): Hmm. (MRS. BASS *enters, equally distraught.*)

MRS. BASS: Forgive the intrusion, Mr. Gray, but . . .

JULIAN (*Brightening*): You've found it?

MRS. BASS: No, sir, I'm afraid not. (*Wringing her hands*) I've had the household looking on their hands and knees for the past hour, sir. (JULIAN *suddenly gets down on hands and knees and looks under the furniture.*) Wherever it's gone to, it appears to be gone for good. (*Noticing him*) Excuse me, Mr. Gray?

JULIAN: Yes?

MRS. BASS: We've already checked down there, sir.

JULIAN (*Emphatically*): It's here somewhere in the house and I want it found.

MRS. BASS: Yes, Mr. Gray. (MISS FINCH *bustles in.*)

JULIAN (*Hopefully*): Ah, Miss Finch! What have you found?

MISS FINCH (*Shaking her head*): Nothing, sir. We've looked in every nook and cranny and combed every cubic foot.

JULIAN (*Hands on hips as he faces them*): I don't think the three of you fully appreciate how grave this situation really is. Now concentrate and try to remember when the last time was that you saw it. (*The three of them exchange uncomfortable glances.*) Well?

HOBBS: Actually, sir—

JULIAN: Yes?

MRS. BASS: We've never seen it at all, Mr. Gray.

JULIAN: What?

MISS FINCH: You kept it hidden under that ugly canvas night and day so we've never even seen it . . .

HOBBS: Which is why we're having so difficult a time searching for something when we haven't a clue what it looks like.

JULIAN (*Exasperated*): But I've told you. It's a picture.

MRS. BASS: A picture of what, sir?

JULIAN: A picture is a picture, Mrs. Bass. Now if any of you finds a picture and it's not any of the pictures you see every day on these walls, then it's probably the one that's lost. Understood? Now, everyone get back to work. Hobbs, help me look in the closet. (*As he exits into closet*) We're going to look until we find it, is that clear?

HOBBS: Yes, sir. (*As HOBBS stands outside closet, a variety of coats, sports equipment, and stuffed animals comes flying out. HOBBS does his best to catch things.*)

MISS FINCH (*To MRS. BASS*): Do you suppose it's quite valuable, this lost picture of his? I've never seen him so upset.

MRS. BASS: Not half as upset as he'll be if we don't get back to looking for it.

MISS FINCH: Did you check with Miss Applegate? Perhaps the picture is upstairs.

MRS. BASS: She should be back any moment from the charity bazaar.

MISS FINCH: What charity bazaar?

MRS. BASS: Oh, it's quite the annual event. Mr. Gray always gathers up his best rummage for it and one of us packs it off for the sale.

MISS FINCH (*A worried look coming over her face*): Oh, dear!

MRS. BASS: What's wrong?

MISS FINCH: You don't suppose that Miss Applegate saw that old canvas and thought—

MRS. BASS: Oh no! (*As they exit*) We'd better ask her the moment she walks in! (*They collide with* EDDIE *as he enters.*)

MISS FINCH (*Quickly dusting him off*): Oh, excuse us, Mr. Eddie!

MRS. BASS: Yes, we're terribly sorry! (*They hurry out, much to* EDDIE's *puzzlement.* EDDIE *sees* HOBBS *at closet and strolls over curiously.*)

JULIAN (*From within*): It has to be here, Hobbs, that's all there is to it. (*Things continue to fly out.*)

HOBBS: Whatever you say, sir.

EDDIE: How's it going, Hobbs?

HOBBS (*Turning to address him*): Not very well, Mr. Eddie. Here to see Mr. Gray, are you? (*A tennis racquet flies out of closet, just missing* HOBBS' *head;* EDDIE *catches it.*)

EDDIE: Amazing! I've been looking for this old thing for years!

JULIAN (*Emerging*): Eddie! What on earth brings you here?

EDDIE: Usually my car. And what do you mean, what am I doing here? Today's the big day, as I recall. Or am I mistaken?

JULIAN (*To* HOBBS): It's not in the closet, Hobbs. You can put those things away.

HOBBS: Very well, sir. (*Disappears into closet*)

JULIAN (*To* EDDIE): A change of plans. I'm afraid today won't do at all.

EDDIE: Cold feet, huh?

JULIAN: Nothing of the sort. I'm just in the middle of something I can't leave.

EDDIE: So what do I do with the flowers, the chocolates, and the limousine you especially asked me to have polished for your date with that mystery woman you're so secretive about?

JULIAN: I'll just have to call and reschedule my proposal of marriage for a less stressful day.

EDDIE: So, what exactly are you in the middle of?

JULIAN (*Distracted*): What?

EDDIE: You seem to be looking for something.

JULIAN (*Thinks a moment, then addresses* EDDIE *confidentially*): Can you keep a secret, Eddie?

EDDIE: Sure.

JULIAN: Good, so can I. (*Continues his search of the room*)

EDDIE: Oh, come on, that's not fair. I tell you all of *my* secrets.

JULIAN: But you don't have any.

EDDIE: But if I did, you're the first person I'd come to. (*Following him*) Come on, give me a hint.

JULIAN: All right, all right. I'm looking for a picture. But that's all I'm going to say.

EDDIE (*Snaps fingers in recognition*): You mean that one of the ugly old guy you keep hidden away in the attic? (*Shocked,* JULIAN *glances around to see if anyone has heard, notices* HOBBS *stepping into the closet and hastily closes the door behind him.*)

JULIAN: How did you know about that?

EDDIE: Well, remember that time you asked me to house-sit when you went to Florida and you told me not to get into anything? (JULIAN *reacts in exasperation.*) So who is it, anyway? A dead ancestor or something?

JULIAN (*Sighing*): You wouldn't believe me if I told you.

EDDIE: Sure I would. I'd even believe it if you said it was you.

JULIAN (*Horrified*): Who said it was me?

EDDIE: You mean it is?

JULIAN (*Cautiously*): What would you say if I said yes?

EDDIE: I'd say you picked a really bad artist. No offense, but it makes you look about a hundred and five.

JULIAN: Eddie, I'm going to tell you something I've never told anyone else. (*Secretly*) That picture has certain—well—properties that make it very important I never misplace it.

EDDIE: Huh? (MRS. BASS, MISS FINCH, *and* MISS APPLEGATE *scurry in.*)

MRS. BASS: Excuse me, Mr. Gray, but I think we may have found it.

JULIAN (*Elated*): You did? That's marvelous!

MISS FINCH: Not quite so marvelous, I'm afraid, sir.

JULIAN: What do you mean?

MISS APPLEGATE: I seem to have blundered, Mr. Gray.

JULIAN: What is it, Miss Applegate? What's wrong?

MISS APPLEGATE: It's about the picture, sir. (*Shakes her head*) I made a terrible mistake.

JULIAN (*Alarmed*): Something's happened to it?

MISS APPLEGATE: I took it to the bazaar with the rest of the rummage.

JULIAN: Oh, dear! Well, we'd better not waste any time. Come on, Eddie, we don't want someone to buy it before we can get there!

MISS APPLEGATE (*Upset*): Someone has already bought it, sir.

JULIAN (*Sinking to sofa*): Oh, no! It's worse than I thought.

EDDIE: Maybe not. They keep records on those things, don't they? (*Explaining*) All I have to do is get the name and address and clear this whole thing up. (*Straightening JULIAN's tie*) You, in the meantime, can keep your date with your secret lady love.

JULIAN: Eddie! That's brilliant. How can I ever thank you?

EDDIE: Hmmm . . . you could start with mentioning me in your will . . . .

JULIAN: I'll consider it when the picture's back safe and sound where it belongs. Let's go; we haven't a second to lose. (*He and* EDDIE *exit, followed by the three women. Curtain*)

* * * * *

SCENE 2

SETTING: *Darla White's garden. Chairs and table have been set out for tea; French doors leading into house are stage right.*

AT RISE: DARLA WHITE *and* CINDY *are looking at a picture on an easel, its back toward the audience.*

DARLA: Well, what do you think?

CINDY (*Wrinkling her nose*): I think that people are going to say, "Darla White, have you lost your mind?"

DARLA: Now, Cindy, be kind.

CINDY: I was. I just don't see what possessed you to buy something so ugly!

DARLA (*Studying it*): I don't know. I think it has a certain charm to it.

CINDY: And what's your Mr. Gray going to say about it?

DARLA: Oh, for heaven's sake, Cindy. He's not *my* Mr. Gray.

CINDY: Well, rumor has it that there's going to be a Mrs. Gray.

DARLA (*Casually*): Oh? Anyone we know? (*They both laugh.*)

CINDY: So, is he coming to call today?

DARLA (*Checking her watch*): Any moment now. (*Scowls*) Hmm . . . he's usually so punctual.

CINDY: Maybe something came up at the gallery. (*Smiles*)

Just imagine, pretty soon you'll be surrounded by Rembrandts, Picassos, and Van Goghs—

DARLA: And Julian! Oh, Cindy, I can't wait for you to meet him.

CINDY: I feel that I already have. If I'm not reading about him in the paper, I'm hearing about him from you.

DARLA: He really is wonderful. There's something that's so old-fashioned and worldly and sweet about Julian that I've never found in anyone else. He just has a way about him that's absolutely timeless!

CINDY: Well, if you don't mind a little advice . . .

DARLA: What?

CINDY (*Indicating picture*): You might want to wait until after you're married before you let him see what terrible taste you have in modern art! (BARTLETT *enters.*)

BARTLETT: Excuse me, Miss White, but Mr. Julian Gray is here to take tea with you.

DARLA (*Smiling*): By all means, Bartlett, please show Mr. Gray to the garden. (*He exits.*)

CINDY: I really was serious about that picture.

DARLA: Well, if you really think so. (*Takes it off easel and hands it to her*) You know where it goes. (CINDY *exits and* JULIAN *enters, but because the picture is facing her body, he doesn't see what it is.*)

JULIAN (*Kissing* DARLA's *hand*): Darla, darling. Forgive me for being late, but something unexpected came up.

DARLA: You're here now, Julian. That's all that really matters.

JULIAN (*Awkwardly*): I hope I'm not speaking out of turn, Darla, but I've been giving our situation some serious thought lately.

DARLA: And?

JULIAN: And I realized that I'd be making a horrible mistake.

DARLA (*Concerned*): A mistake?

JULIAN: I'm afraid I haven't been completely honest with you.

DARLA: You can tell me anything, Julian. You know that.

JULIAN (*Pacing as he talks*): Yes, but what if I were to tell you that—well, that I'm a little bit older than I look?

DARLA (*Laughing*): Silly man! What does age have to do with anything?

JULIAN: Well, what if I told you that I might never change?

DARLA: Then I'd have no complaints in the world. You're perfect just as you are, Julian.

JULIAN: Let me put it another way, then. What would you say if, hypothetically, of course, someone had a picture of himself and every year the picture got older but the person himself never aged a day?

DARLA (*Musing*): I'd say that was very odd.

JULIAN: Well, then, what if I were also to say—

BARTLETT (*Entering*): Excuse me, Miss White, but there's a gentleman here to see you.

DARLA: This isn't a good time, Bartlett.

BARTLETT: He says it's most urgent and refuses to go away.

DARLA (*Perplexed*): Did he give a name? (*Before* BART-LETT *can reply,* EDDIE *barges in, but does not see* JULIAN.)

EDDIE (*To* DARLA): Hi, sorry to barge in. Listen, you don't know me, but this morning you bought a picture that belongs to someone else and he's really anxious to get it back as soon as possible, so whatever you paid for it, he'll be glad to pay you double for it.

JULIAN (*Loudly, through clenched teeth, to silence him*): Eddie!

EDDIE (*Completely surprised*): Hey, what are you doing here? I thought you went to see your mystery—(*Realizing*) uh-oh . . .

DARLA: Julian, do you know this person?

JULIAN: Well, er . . . uh . . .

DARLA: You must know him—you called him Eddie. (*To EDDIE*) Is that your name?

EDDIE (*Helplessly*): Uh—lucky guess. (*Looks at watch*) Wow! Look at the time. I'd better be going. (*Turns to go*)

DARLA: Wait a minute. You said something about a picture.

EDDIE: I did? I really must be going now. I'm sorry to have bothered you, Ms. White. (*CINDY enters.*)

CINDY: Is it too late to join the party?

DARLA: Cindy, this is Eddie. He's interested in the picture I just bought.

CINDY (*Incredulously*): Really? Have you seen it?

EDDIE (*Stammering*): Well, I—

DARLA: Would you two excuse us?

EDDIE *and* CINDY: Sure. Of course. (*They begin to mime conversation, as* JULIAN *and* DARLA *step downstage.*)

DARLA (*To* JULIAN): And you were talking about a picture as well.

JULIAN (*Innocently*): Was I?

DARLA: Julian, is there something you're not telling me?

JULIAN (*With a heavy sigh*): Yes, I'm afraid there is.

DARLA: Well?

JULIAN: It's about the picture you bought at the bazaar this morning.

DARLA: What about it?

JULIAN: I was trying to tell you earlier. (*Glances over at* EDDIE *and* CINDY, *who are engrossed in conversation*) For openers, I should start by telling you who Eddie really is.

DARLA: Who, then?

JULIAN: Eddie is my grandson, Darla. And I'm—well, I'm actually a hundred and five years old. You see, that old man in the picture you bought is actually me. It was done a long time ago at this quaint little shop on 45th Street run by a curious little artist named—

DARLA: Mr. Lim.

JULIAN: Yes, Mr. Lim, and—(*Suddenly; surprised*) how do you know about Mr. Lim?

DARLA (*Crossing to put her arm in his*): Because, my dear sweet Julian, the picture of you is hanging upstairs next to the picture he did of me.

JULIAN (*Surprised*): You mean you're—

DARLA: A hundred and two on my birthday next April. (*Pointing upstage to* CINDY) Cindy is actually my great-niece.

JULIAN: You're kidding.

DARLA: Is this the face of a woman who lies?

JULIAN: No, certainly not.

DARLA: I guess we're just a couple of oldies but goodies.

JULIAN: Well, I think we're picture perfect! (*They laugh and exit as curtain falls.*)

THE END

PRODUCTION NOTES

PICTURE PERFECT

Characters: 4 male; 5 female.

Playing Time: 20 minutes.

Costumes: Julian and Eddie both wear formal attire. Mrs. Bass, Miss Finch, and Miss Applegate wear maids' uniforms. Hobbs and Bartlett wear dark butler suits. Darla wears elegant tea dress. Cindy wears less formal dress.

Properties: Feather duster, coats, sports equipment, stuffed animals and tennis racquet in closet; painting and easel.

Setting: Scene 1: Elegant drawing room of Julian's house, filled with many sculptures; several paintings are hung on walls. Sofa, chair, and coffee table are center stage; needlepoint pillows are on both sofa and chair. Down right is a large potted plant and an umbrella stand. Upstage right is a closet with working door. Upstage left are double doors. Scene 2: Darla White's garden. Chairs and table have been set out for tea; French doors leading into house are stage right.

Sound and lighting: No special effects.

Once Upon a Fairy Tale

Characters

AGNES
MATILDA } *fairy tale witches*
BLANCHE
SNOW WHITE
SLEEPING BEAUTY
PRINCE CHARMING
HANSEL
GRETEL
OFFICER MALONEY, *police officer*
ERNIE, *owner of Ernie's Diner*
BRUNO
MAX
MRS. GILROY
MRS. SPENSE
FREDDIE SPENSE, *her son*

SCENE 1

TIME: *The present.*
SETTING: *Picture book scene. The stage is very dark. There are several cardboard trees to the left and right. A large cardboard rock is center.*
AT RISE: *Thunder sound effects and eerie music play as a*

squabble of voices is heard off right. Bobbing light of flash-lights precedes AGNES, MATILDA, *and* BLANCHE *as they enter. All are in traditional garb but have distinctively different personalities.* AGNES *carries apple,* MATILDA *drags broom, and* BLANCHE *primps in hand mirror.*

AGNES: Hurry up, you two. We haven't got all night!

MATILDA: Are you sure this is the way?

BLANCHE (*Sarcastically*): Of course she's sure. Miss Know-It-All knows *everything!*

MATILDA (*Suddenly*): Sh-h-h! What was that?

BLANCHE: Just a bat! Don't be such a ninny.

MATILDA (*Worried*): I don't know, Agnes. None of this looks familiar to me. Maybe we should think this through some more.

BLANCHE: We've thought it to death, Matilda. It's now or never.

AGNES: For once, I agree with Blanche. If we stay, it'll be the same thing over and over and over again. (*Bites into apple*)

BLANCHE: Hey! That's my apple!

MATILDA: Besides, do you think you should be eating that now? What if they don't have food where we're going?

BLANCHE: Of course they have food. (*Primps*) But more important, they have beauty pageants. And I intend to win every single one. (*To mirror*) Isn't that right, Mirror? (*Silence.* AGNES *and* MATILDA *laugh;* BLANCHE *glares and shouts.*) Mirror! How would you like to have seven years of bad luck, you silly piece of glass? (*Offstage murmur of voices and scuffle of feet are heard.*)

AGNES (*Looking off in alarm*): Oh, no, they're coming!

BLANCHE: Well, don't just stand there, Agnes, which way do we go?

AGNES (*Looking off left, pointing*): Over there! Just below that sign that says "The End"! (AGNES *and* BLANCHE *start to run;* MATILDA *follows, but looks back anxiously.*)

BLANCHE (*Sternly*): Matilda, hurry up!

MATILDA (*Worried*): You don't think this is an awfully mean thing to do?

BLANCHE (*Simply*): The meanest. That's why we're doing it. (*She and AGNES rush back to grab MATILDA and start pulling her.*) Now, come on.

AGNES: We'd better go before they catch us! (*They exit. Several people in pursuit rush on right. PRINCE CHARMING holds lantern high, as he leads on SNOW WHITE, SLEEPING BEAUTY, HANSEL, and GRETEL. Stage is partially illuminated but not bright enough to see backdrop behind them: a large-scale open book of fairy tales.*)

SNOW WHITE: Whatever possessed them to take off like that?

BEAUTY: Matilda was just about to show me how to use her spinning wheel.

GRETEL: Agnes was going to push Hansel into a little cage.

SNOW: And Blanche had just offered me the most tempting apple, when, all of a sudden, she tossed it to Agnes and away they ran!

PRINCE (*Impatiently*): It sounds like another crazy prank to me. We'll just have to wait until they come back.

GRETEL (*Suddenly pointing upstage*): Oh, no!

HANSEL: What is it, Gretel?

GRETEL: Look! Up there! (*PRINCE holds lantern higher, illuminating stage. All turn to stare at huge illustrated page of story and characters. In the scene, distinctly accented by white silhouettes, are cutouts of witches in pointed hats, indicating their escape from book.*)

SNOW: Oh, no! Where could they have gone?

BEAUTY: Maybe someone has stolen them.

PRINCE (*Walking short distance away; pointing to ground, calling*): Hansel, Gretel, come here! (*They exit.*)

BEAUTY: It just doesn't make sense.

SNOW: Especially when things were going so well. (PRINCE, HANSEL, *and* GRETEL *return, carrying apple core, a mirror, and a broom.*)

PRINCE: I'm afraid I have some bad news. (*All gather around him.*) They've gone *out there.* (*All gasp.*)

SNOW (*Wide-eyed*): You don't mean—

BEAUTY: I can't bear to think of it!

GRETEL: Should we go after them?

HANSEL: Good idea! Let's go!

PRINCE: Wait a minute. We can't.

BEAUTY: Why not?

PRINCE: Because we all live happily ever after. Everyone knows that. It wouldn't be fair to run off.

GRETEL (*Angrily*): But *they* did! And right in mid-story.

PRINCE: But they're witches. They have special powers that we don't.

SNOW: Oh, you're right. I forgot about that. *But,* if they're loose somewhere OUT THERE—

PRINCE (*Suddenly*): Then they're as powerless as we are. Once they stepped out of these pages, their powers were lost.

BEAUTY (*Brightly*): Well, there's no sense in being gloomy, is there? We have the rest of our lives to get on with!

PRINCE (*Sighing*): I'm afraid that brings up other bad news. (*Points to book behind them*) Our stories can't go on until they return.

SNOW (*Exasperated*): What? You mean I'm going to have to keep cooking and cleaning for those dwarfs forever and ever?

GRETEL: And Hansel and I won't be able to rescue the gingerbread kids?

BEAUTY: Will I have to sit in front of a spinning wheel day in and day out without a clue how it works?

PRINCE: You're not the only one who's upset, Beauty. If they don't come back, I'll never get to give you a kiss so you can wake up. (SNOW *clears her throat and folds her arms; he hastily addresses her.*) Or you either, Snow.

GRETEL: So what do we do?

PRINCE: The only thing we *can* do—sit and wait and hope that they come to their senses. (*They sit as lights dim and curtain closes.*)

* * * * *

SCENE 2

SETTING: *City street. There is sign reading* NO LOITERING *at one side.*

BEFORE RISE: *Loud screech of brakes and sounds of traffic horns and ad libbed shouting are heard. In front of curtain,* AGNES, MATILDA, *and* BLANCHE, *somewhat disheveled, run onstage.*

AGNES: Whew! That was a close one! That car barely missed us.

BLANCHE (*Annoyed*): It wouldn't have been so close if a certain party hadn't left her broom at home.

MATILDA (*Indignantly*): I didn't leave it at home, I dropped it! Besides, it's only a two-seater . . . and guess who I would have left behind?

AGNES: Will you two stop bickering? We've got to take stock of our situation and find some food.

MATILDA (*Matter-of-factly to* AGNES): I told you that you shouldn't have eaten your apple.

BLANCHE: For your information, that was *my* apple she ate.

AGNES: You mean Snow White's, don't you?

BLANCHE (*Blankly*): Who? (*Chuckles*) There, you see! I've forgotten them already!

MATILDA: Do you think they miss us?

AGNES: If they do, it's their own fault.

MATILDA (*Hopefully*): Do you think they'll try to find us?

BLANCHE (*Matter-of-factly*): They can't. We're here, and they're back there.

MATILDA: But what about the stories?

AGNES: Oh, Matilda, we've been over this a thousand times. The stories no longer exist.

BLANCHE: And little children all over the world will have to go to bed without hearing them. . . . And *we'll* live happily ever after! (*She and* AGNES *cackle.*)

MATILDA: Speaking of living—

AGNES: Yes?

MATILDA: Where are we supposed to stay?

BLANCHE (*Blandly*): In the nearest castle, of course. When we find one, that is.

AGNES: Let's look for one after lunch. I'm hungry.

MATILDA (*Puzzled*): Then why don't you just conjure up some food? A few crunchy batwings, perhaps? Maybe a chocolate-covered lizard?

AGNES (*Ill at ease*): Well . . . uh . . .

MATILDA: What's wrong?

AGNES (*Offering quick explanation*): Magnetic fields. They seem to be interfering with my spells at the moment. (*Snaps fingers*) I know! Why don't you turn yourself into a raven and go scouting ahead for us?

MATILDA (*Uncomfortable*): Uh . . . my arms are kind of tired. Besides, all this walking is good for us. (BLANCHE *has been bobbing up and down as if she's trying to catch a glimpse of something.*)

AGNES: What are you doing, Blanche?

BLANCHE (*Frustrated*): I'm trying to catch my reflection in one of those shiny things that nearly hit us.

MATILDA: Where's your mirror?

BLANCHE (*Uneasily*): I seem to have misplaced it.

AGNES: Can't you zap up another one?

BLANCHE (*Defensively*): I prefer to save my magic for more important things. (OFFICER MALONEY *enters.*)

MALONEY: Hey, you three in the Halloween costumes!

MATILDA (*Puzzled*): Is that man talking to us? (*Witches look around.*)

AGNES: He must mean someone else. (MALONEY *clears throat and folds arms.*)

MATILDA (*Pleasantly*): Hello.

MALONEY: Do you care to explain what you three are doing? Can't you read that sign? (*Points*)

BLANCHE: Of course we can read the sign. We can also speak seven languages, including toad and fish.

MALONEY: Yeah, well the one up there's in English, and it says, "No Loitering." If you stay here, I'm going to have to turn you in.

BLANCHE: Turn us into what?

MALONEY (*Annoyed*): Do you three have any I.D.'s on you?

AGNES: I beg your pardon?

MALONEY (*Irritated*): Identification.

AGNES (*Laughing*): Don't be ridiculous. Why would we need *that?* Everybody knows who we are.

MALONEY (*Sarcastically*): You want to let me in on this secret and tell me your last names?

MATILDA (*Proudly*): Bewitched, Bothered, and Bewildered.

MALONEY: Sure. And I'm Peter Pan.

MATILDA (*Laughing*): Oh, go on! Peter's much younger.

MALONEY (*Exasperated*): Look, I'm going to say this only once. Scram. I don't want to see you still here when I get back. (*Starts to exit*)

BLANCHE: Excuse me? (*He turns.*) Perhaps you could tell us where to find the nearest beauty pageant.

MALONEY (*Dubious*): You three are looking for a beauty pageant?

BLANCHE: Oh, not them. (*Bats eyelashes*) Just me. (MALONEY *doubles up in laughter.*)

MALONEY: That's the funniest thing I've ever heard!

BLANCHE (*Rolling up her sleeves, hands on hips*): How would you like to be a 300-pound snail?

MATILDA: Now, Blanche, don't lose your temper.

BLANCHE: Out of my way, Matilda. (*Waves arms and chants*) Abracadabra, take this male, turn him into an overgrown snail! (*Nothing happens. Embarrassed, she smiles sheepishly.*) Just a little joke.

MALONEY (*Shaking his head*): Californians . . . (*Exits*)

MATILDA: Blanche, what happened?

BLANCHE: I decided not to cause a scene.

MATILDA: Obviously, something isn't working out here. And until we find out what happened to our powers, we'll have to try to fit in.

BLANCHE: Fit in as what?

MATILDA: As humans. (*Explains*) We'll have to get jobs and earn money and find a place to live.

AGNES: Get jobs? All we know how to do is be witches.

MATILDA: Well, it's worth a try, isn't it?

BLANCHE (*As they exit*): Something tells me I'm going to hate it.

* * *

SETTING: *Ernie's Diner, a tacky, greasy eatery. Plastic tablecloths cover tables center; counter and kitchen are left. Street exit is up right; door to storage room is up left.*

AT RISE: ERNIE *is leaning over counter reading paper as witches enter;* MATILDA *carries* HELP WANTED *sign.*

MATILDA: Hello? Anybody home?

ERNIE: You're a little early for trick-or-treat.

AGNES: Are you the one who needs help?

ERNIE (*Looking them over*): Not from the looks of it. What are you three supposed to be?

MATILDA (*Showing the sign*): Your new employees.

ERNIE: Employee singular. I've got only one job.

ALL (*Together*): We'll take it.

AGNES (*Explaining*): We work as a team.

BLANCHE: Yes, you might say it's our life story.

ERNIE (*Skeptical*): Do you have any recent experience?

MATILDA: Doing what?

ERNIE: Look, I want someone who can work magic in this kitchen, fly around the dining room, and turn that register into a goldmine. If you can't do that—

BLANCHE (*Brightly*): Oh, but we can! We've had experience, that is.

MATILDA: Blanche—

BLANCHE (*Whispering to other two*): He said recent, not current.

AGNES (*To* MATILDA): Once our powers come back, it'll be a breeze.

BLANCHE: And once my powers come back, I'm giving notice.

AGNES (*To* ERNIE): We'll take it.

ERNIE: Yes, well, as I said, I'm paying only one salary.

MATILDA: We'll split it three ways. Anything is better than having to go back where we came from.

ERNIE (*Suspiciously*): Oh, yeah? And where's that? (*Witches look at each other for an answer.*)

AGNES: Oh, it's not important.

BLANCHE: Just consider it a closed chapter in our lives.

ERNIE: You three aren't fugitives, are you? (*They shake their heads.*) Are you sure no one's after you?

BLANCHE: Absolutely positive.

ERNIE: Good. (*Checks watch*) The lunch crowd's going to be

coming in any second. (*Points upstage*) You can change into your uniforms in there. (*They start to exit.*) And make it snappy! (*They exit just as* BRUNO *and* MAX, *two construction workers, enter.*)

BRUNO: Yo, Ernie!

ERNIE: What d'you say, Bruno? Hey, Max! (*They sit at counter.*)

MAX: How 'bout those 49ers?

ERNIE: Looking good, looking good. You boys need some menus?

BRUNO: Not me. I've got a hankering for an onion burger and all the works.

MAX: And throw in a side of fries.

ERNIE: Whoa! Save it for the new girls I hired.

MAX: What happened to Dolores?

ERNIE: Aw, she's out in Hollywood trying to be a movie star. (*Witches reenter with aprons tied around their black dresses, and waitress caps over the front of their hats.*)

BRUNO (*Not yet seeing them*): Well, Dolores sure has got the looks to be the next Miss America.

BLANCHE (*Hearing him, flattered; strolling up to counter*): Why, thank you. Have we met? (BRUNO *and* MAX *gasp in shock as she extends her hand.*) I'm Blanche.

ERNIE (*Annoyed*): Forget the socializing and take their order. (*Witches form assembly line to take order.*)

BRUNO: Double onion burger—

BLANCHE (*To* MATILDA): Double onion burger—(MATILDA *repeats this to* AGNES, *who repeats it to* ERNIE.)

MAX: Make that two. (*Repeat sequence*)

BRUNO: Pickle, lettuce, tomato—(*Repeat sequence*)

MAX: Hold the mayo. (*Repeat sequence*)

BRUNO: Chocolate shake—

ERNIE (*Gritting teeth*): Wait! Nobody says another word!

MATILDA: Is something wrong?

ERNIE (*Shouting*): Yes! (*Calms down*) You (*Points to MA-TILDA*)—get back there and start cooking. (*She goes left. To* AGNES) You serve it when it's ready.

BLANCHE (*As* MRS. GILROY *enters*): What do *I* do?

ERNIE (*Pointing*): And you stop scaring the customers!

MRS. GILROY: Excuse me?

BLANCHE (*Turning to face her*): Yes? (MRS. GILROY *gasps a scream;* BLANCHE *quickly addresses* ERNIE.) I didn't do a thing!

ERNIE (*Wearily*): Just take the orders, that's all I ask. (*Exits upstage as* BLANCHE *shows* MRS. GILROY *to a table;* MAX *and* BRUNO *quietly converse.*)

BLANCHE (*Pulling out a notebook and pencil*): What will it be?

MRS. GILROY: May I see a menu?

BLANCHE (*Pointing at counter*): There's one over there. (MRS. GILROY *looks annoyed.*) Oh, you mean you want to see one over here? No problem. (*Snaps her fingers at menu, but nothing happens. Calls to* MATILDA) Matilda, bring me that menu!

MATILDA: I can't, Blanche. I'm cooking.

BLANCHE: Agnes?

AGNES: I'm waiting to serve.

BRUNO (*Shouting*): Hey! Let's see some food over here!

MAX: Yeah! We don't have all day! (BLANCHE *trudges over to get the menu and brings it back, hands it to* MRS. GILROY.)

MRS. GILROY: The tuna looks nice.

BLANCHE (*Writing*): One tuna . . .

MRS. GILROY: Is that on white or wheat?

BLANCHE: Wheat.

MRS. GILROY: I think I'll have turkey.

BLANCHE (*Crossing it out*): Turkey on wheat . . .

MRS. GILROY: No, make that on white. What's the soup?

BLANCHE: Lentil surprise.

MRS. GILROY: I think I'll have a salad.

BLANCHE (*Crossing it out again*): O.K., one salad.

MRS. GILROY: On second thought, I'll have the soup. What kind was it again? (MRS. SPENSE *and* FREDDIE *enter;* FREDDIE *carries a big book under his arm.*)

BLANCHE: Why don't you decide, and I'll come back. (*As* MRS. SPENSE *and* FREDDIE *sit*) May I take your order?

FREDDIE (*Looking up and smiling at* BLANCHE): Good afternoon, ma'am.

BLANCHE (*Taken aback by his friendliness*): Er—afternoon to you, too.

MRS. SPENSE: What would you like to drink, Freddie, dear?

FREDDIE: A glass of water is fine, Mama.

MRS. SPENSE: But you're a growing boy, Freddie. Besides, it's a long train ride to Seattle. (*To* BLANCHE) My husband just got a new job.

BLANCHE (*Looking him over*): My friend Agnes has some good gingerbread cookies back there.

FREDDIE (*Politely*): No, thank you, ma'am. Mama says too many sweets are bad for your teeth.

MRS. SPENSE: I'd like a cup of coffee. How about some soup, Freddie?

FREDDIE (*To* BLANCHE): What's the soup today, ma'am?

BLANCHE: Lentil surprise.

FREDDIE: Yes, please. And that's a very nice dress, ma'am.

BLANCHE (*Awkwardly*): Uh, why, thank you. (*A crash is heard from kitchen.*)

MATILDA: Oh, dear!

BRUNO (*Pounding fist on table*): We're starving! Where's our grub?

AGNES (*To* MATILDA): Oh, throw it back on the plate—

they'll never notice. (*She and* MATILDA *proceed to camouflage plate of food with ketchup and large sprigs of parsley. The scene downstage continues.*)

MRS. GILROY: Oh, waitress, waitress! I think I'm ready to order.

BLANCHE (*To* MRS. SPENSE): Excuse me.

FREDDIE: Would you read me a story, Mama? (*Holds out his book*)

MRS. SPENSE: Oh, Freddie, I've told you before—I can't.

FREDDIE (*Frowning*): But why not?

MRS. SPENSE: Because the stories aren't there anymore.

FREDDIE: But they were there last night. (AGNES *delivers food to* BRUNO *and* MAX, *passing by* MRS. SPENSE's *table on her return.*)

MRS. SPENSE: I wish I had an answer, dear. (*Sighs*) And I wish you hadn't carried that big book all this way for nothing.

FREDDIE: But it's my favorite.

MRS. SPENSE: Yes, but you saw for yourself, honey. The pages are all empty now.

AGNES: Pardon me, but what's that book?

MRS. SPENSE: Oh, it's just a bunch of blank pages now.

FREDDIE: But it was the best book in the whole world.

MATILDA (*Listening*): What happened?

MRS. SPENSE: The stories and pictures just vanished.

FREDDIE: But they'll be back, Mama!

BLANCHE (*Curious*): What will be back?

FREDDIE: The stories, ma'am. They're all about princes and magic and witches—

MATILDA (*Excitedly*): And what?

FREDDIE: Witches, ma'am. They're the most important part of the whole book.

AGNES (*Touched*): We are? (*Quickly*) I mean—they are?

MRS. SPENSE: Without them, no one would appreciate the

happily-ever-afters. (*Smiles*) Well, we're interrupting their work, Freddie.

FREDDIE: Oh, I'm sorry, ma'am. I wouldn't want you to get in trouble.

MRS. GILROY (*Impatiently*): Are you going to take my order or not?

BLANCHE: In a minute. (*To* AGNES *and* MATILDA) I think we need to talk, girls. (*To* FREDDIE) Uh, would you mind if I borrowed your book for a second?

FREDDIE (*Handing her the book*): Go ahead, ma'am. (*Three cross downstage; behind them, the scene dims as curtain slowly closes.*)

BLANCHE: You know, I've been thinking—

MATILDA: Have you been thinking what I've been thinking?

AGNES: What's that?

MATILDA: It sure would be nice to hear the sound of my old spinning wheel again . . . .

BLANCHE: It must be awfully boring for Mirror to have no one to talk to . . . .

AGNES: I suddenly have a craving for gingerbread . . . .

BLANCHE: Why don't we just admit we made a mistake?

AGNES: Never! (*Shrugs*) Though it would be fun to see what the old gang has been up to.

MATILDA: Aren't you the one who said we'd never go back?

AGNES: Now, now, Matilda. Never is a long time.

MATILDA: But what if they don't want us?

BLANCHE: Nonsense. You heard what that little boy said. We're the most important part of the whole book.

MATILDA (*Pointing to book*): But how do we get back? We've never done this before, Blanche.

BLANCHE (*Sighing deeply*): There's a first time for everything.

AGNES (*Snapping fingers*): Time! That's it! Isn't there something about time at the beginning of every story?

BLANCHE: Yes, I remember the spell—(*Looks at others*) It's worth a try. (*Waving hand over book*)
Round about the pages go,
Bats that squeal and winds that blow,
Take us back in witches' rhyme
To "Once upon a magic time."
(*She snaps book closed; lights black out as voices are heard over mike.*)

ERNIE: Hey, where did those three waitresses go?

BRUNO: I hope you can find 'em.

MAX: Yeah, I want to order seconds. This is the best lunch I ever had.

MRS. GILROY: Is someone going to take my order or not?

FREDDIE (*Excitedly*): Mama, look!

MRS. SPENSE: What is it, Freddie?

FREDDIE: My book—the stories are back!

MRS. SPENSE: But Freddie, that's impossi—(*After a pause*) Oh, my goodness! You're right! (*Curtain opens slowly to reveal* SNOW, BEAUTY, PRINCE, HANSEL, *and* GRETEL *sitting in the same huddle as before, on darkened stage.*)

HANSEL: I wonder where they are right now.

GRETEL: They may as well be a million miles away.

PRINCE: Oh, come on, cheer up, kids. It's not as bad as that.

SNOW: Really?

PRINCE: No, I just said that to make them feel better.

BEAUTY: I feel as if we've been sitting here for a hundred years! (*Yawns*) I could use a good nap.

PRINCE: We just can't give up hope, gang! (*There is a loud crash offstage; they all jump and listen. Witches stumble on stage.*)

MATILDA: Are you sure you know what you're doing?

AGNES: It wasn't my idea to leave in the first place.

BLANCHE: Oh, apple-sap, it was, too!

GRETEL: They're back! (*She and* HANSEL *rush to hug them.*)

SNOW: We were so worried!

BEAUTY: Are you O.K.?

PRINCE: You're a sight for sore eyes!

HANSEL: It's been terrible without you!

GRETEL: Do you mind getting back to work right away?

BLANCHE (*Scratching her head*): Where did we leave off?

SNOW (*Coming forward to take* BLANCHE's *arm*): Well, you had disguised yourself as an apple peddler and had come to offer me a poisoned apple. (*They exit.*)

BEAUTY (*Coming forward to take* MATILDA): And I can hardly wait to learn how to work that spinning wheel.

MATILDA: Oh, it's easy, dear. Come on, I'll show you. (*They exit.*)

PRINCE: And don't forget the spell where I get to kiss her so she'll wake up! (*Exits.* HANSEL *and* GRETEL *grab* AGNES *by the hand.*)

GRETEL: Can we go to the gingerbread house now?

HANSEL: And eat all the shingles off your roof?

AGNES (*Curious*): Did you really miss us?

GRETEL: Of course we did. (AGNES *crooks a finger at them.*)

AGNES: You know what?

HANSEL *and* GRETEL (*Leaning forward in suspense*): What? (AGNES *waves arms and gives a loud cackle. Terrified,* HANSEL *and* GRETEL *run off, screaming.* AGNES *smiles knowingly at audience.*)

AGNES: I really love this job. (*Continues her wild cackling as she runs off. Lights slowly come up to reveal the "complete" page of the book, the witches having returned to the empty spots.*)

THE END

PRODUCTION NOTES

ONCE UPON A FAIRY TALE

Characters: 8 female, 7 male.

Playing Time: 35 minutes.

Costumes: Witches, traditional garb. Agnes wears black wig; Matilda, gray wig; Blanche, blonde wig and beauty mark. Storybook characters, appropriate costumes. Officer Maloney, uniform. Ernie, sloppy chef's outfit. Bruno and Max, jeans, t-shirts, hard-hats. Mrs. Gilroy, flowered dress and hat. Mrs. Spense, casual clothes. Freddie, pants and shirt.

Properties: Flashlights; broom; apple; lantern; apple core; hand mirror; HELP WANTED sign; menu; food; large book of fairytales; sports page; aprons; caps; small notebook, pencil.

Setting: Scene 1, picture book scene, with cardboard trees left and right and large cardboard rock center. To right or left is a large cardboard storybook page with a scene of the witches. Their forms are cut out of the page and outlined in white. Scene 2, Before Rise, City street. Sign reading NO LOITERING is at one side. At Rise, Ernie's Diner, a tacky, greasy eatery. Plastic tablecloths cover tables center; a counter and kitchen are left. Street exit is up right; door to storage room is up left.

Lighting: Blackouts.

Sound: Thunder, eerie music, microphoned voices, backstage crash.

The Wedding Bell Blues

Characters

LUCY JACKSON, *owner of Hearts and Flowers*
AGNES, *her secretary*
FRANÇOIS, *the chef*
DAPHNE, *the dressmaker*
BEATRICE, *the florist*
FREDDIE, *a chauffeur*

TIME: *The present, a Friday morning in Spring.*
SETTING: *All action takes place in the receptionist area of Hearts and Flowers, a wedding service whose proud motto displayed on the wall reads,* YOU GET THE GROOM . . . AND WE DO THE REST. *The color scheme is pink and white, festooned with hearts, bells, cherubs, etc. Agnes's desk is center; entry door to office is right, hallway to adjoining offices is left.*
AT RISE: AGNES *is alone in office and is rapidly typing. Phone rings.*
AGNES (*Cheerfully*): Good morning. Hearts and Flowers. This is Agnes. (*Forces politeness*) Yes, Miss Chippendale. That's right, Miss Chippendale. Two hundred more? But Miss Chippendale—(*Scribbles a note to herself*) Yes, I know, Miss Chippendale, but—(LUCY *enters through main door, carrying neat white boxes tied with pink rib-*

bons; she pauses to listen to conversation.) Of course, Miss Chippendale, but—No, Miss Chippendale. Whatever you say, Miss Chippendale. (*Hangs up*)

LUCY: Let me guess—Miss Chippendale, right?

AGNES: Oh, Lucy, you'll never guess what she's gone and done now!

LUCY: Nothing the woman does surprises me any more. What is it this time? (*Sets down her boxes*)

AGNES: She wants 200 more invitations to go out.

LUCY: But that's impossible! The wedding is tomorrow afternoon! There's no way the post office can deliver them.

AGNES: She wants them delivered by hand.

LUCY (*Sighing heavily*): Well, I guess I'll just have to tell the messengers—(AGNES *shakes her head.*) What's wrong?

AGNES: Bad news, Lucy. The messengers called this morning and quit. Temporarily.

LUCY: All of them? And what do you mean by temporarily?

AGNES: They said they'll come back on Monday morning.

LUCY (*Exasperated*): But the wedding is tomorrow!

AGNES: The way Miss Chippendale has been running everyone ragged, you'd think she owns the place.

LUCY: Well, I guess we'll just have to manage somehow, Agnes. This is the biggest client I've ever had.

AGNES (*Helpfully*): I'm free this evening if you need me to work late—would that help?

LUCY (*Relieved*): You're an angel, Agnes! Thank you so much! Here are the decorations for the reception hall. Would you mind dropping them off for me? (*Picks up packages*)

AGNES: No problem. It's on my way to the printers. (*Gathers up her jacket and purse*) Honestly, that woman is so greedy—I bet she's only doing this to get 200 more gifts! (*Exits.* FRANÇOIS *scurries in from hallway.*)

FRANÇOIS: Mademoiselle Jackson!

LUCY (*Looking up from list*): What's wrong, François? You look upset.

FRANÇOIS: It is ze Chippendale wedding, Mademoiselle! Zat bride is—how do you say—crazy!

LUCY: Yes, François, crazy is the right word. What has she done now?

FRANÇOIS: Ze cake! She changes her mind once again! Impossible!

LUCY: I thought she said chocolate was perfect.

FRANÇOIS: Chocolate, four layers. Magnifique, I say! Then she says, "No, François—vanilla, eight layers."

LUCY: Oh, François, I'm so sorry.

FRANÇOIS (*Continuing*): I shrug and start to work on vanilla, eight layers. Within an hour, she changes her mind again! A carrot cake, she says, and ten layers high. (*Warns*) One more call from Mademoiselle Chippendale, and I quit (*Snaps fingers*) just like that! (*Exits*)

LUCY (*Calling after him*): But François—(*Sighs*) Well, I can't really blame him. She's the most impossible client I've ever had! (DAPHNE *enters, crying. She wears a tape measure around her neck and is dragging in yards of satin material.*) Daphne, what's wrong?

DAPHNE: She hates it, Miss Jackson. She absolutely hates it!

LUCY: Who? Wait, don't tell me—it's Miss Chippendale, isn't it?

DAPHNE: First she wants a train, then she doesn't. Then she wants long sleeves, then she wants short.

LUCY: But you do such beautiful work—and the wedding is tomorrow! What does she want now?

DAPHNE: Now she wants silk instead of satin! I like working for you, Miss Jackson, really I do. But if she calls one more time, I'm going to go home sick and not come back until all of this is over! (*Sobs and retreats to hallway, material in tow*)

LUCY: The biggest client I've ever had, and I'm about to lose my best employees because of her! Maybe I never should have taken this assignment. (BEATRICE *runs in, carrying armfuls of flowers and leaving a trail of petals.*) Why, Beatrice! Calm down—what is it?

BEATRICE (*Sniffing*): Oh, Miss Jackson, I don't know where to begin. It's all so horrible!

LUCY (*Concerned*): Has something happened to the flowers?

BEATRICE: Oh, the flowers are fine, but I'm about to fall apart!

LUCY: Why do I have the feeling this has something to do with the Chippendale wedding?

BEATRICE: A few changes now and then, I don't mind, Miss Jackson, but this is ridiculous.

LUCY: Calm down—let's take it from the beginning.

BEATRICE: Well, first she wants daisies and then she wants carnations. And then a spray of daffodils, and I order the daffodils. Then she calls and says she wants roses. (*Shakes her head*) She's impossible!

LUCY: Yes, yes, I know. She's giving all of us a difficult time.

BEATRICE: Well, it's the last time she's changed her mind about the flowers, Miss Jackson. If she calls me once more, she can pick them herself! (*Exits*)

LUCY: Oh, terrific. No cake, no dress, and now, no flowers. I guess all I can do is cross my fingers and hope that nothing else goes wrong. (FREDDIE *enters, wearing a chauffeur's uniform and dark glasses.*) Oh, no, don't tell me you're quitting, too?

FREDDIE (*Removing dark glasses*): I beg your pardon?

LUCY (*Surprised*): Oh, you don't work for me!

FREDDIE: Uh, no, I'm—uh—sort of lost.

LUCY: Where are you headed?

FREDDIE: Oh, it's pretty remote. Not many people would know.

LUCY: Try me.

FREDDIE: Springwater Falls. It's a little place up in—

LUCY: You're kidding me! I used to go up there with my dad all the time!

FREDDIE (*Pleased*): You did?

LUCY: Sure! The fishing's terrific, and there isn't a soul for miles around.

FREDDIE: Yeah, that's it! Do you know how to get there?

LUCY (*Crossing around behind desk*): I can draw you a map.

FREDDIE: Great, I'd appreciate it.

LUCY: No problem. (*Notices his uniform*) Although you're not exactly dressed for fishing.

FREDDIE (*Looking down at his uniform*): Well, I get the weekend off, and I could hardly wait to get started. My gear and stuff are already in the car.

LUCY: I envy you. The weather should be perfect up at the lake and—(*Commotion in the hallway as FRANÇOIS, DAPHNE, and BEATRICE enter together. As they pass the desk, FRANÇOIS throws down his chef's hat, DAPHNE throws down the material, and BEATRICE throws down her flowers. They all march out and close the door.*) Oh, no!

FREDDIE (*Confused*): This may seem an odd thing to ask, but what was all of that about? Some kind of parade?

LUCY (*Upset*): No, what you just saw was the end of my career as a wedding coordinator. Those were my best employees.

FREDDIE: A wedding coordinator? What do you do?

LUCY (*Shrugging*): Everything except get the groom. That's our motto. We take care of the invitations, the cake, the dress, the flowers.

FREDDIE: What does the bride do?

LUCY: She just tells us what she wants. Which, in this case, is the impossible.

FREDDIE: How so?

LUCY: Well, because she's pushy and bossy and orders everyone around as if they're her personal servants.

FREDDIE: Why did you take a client like that in the first place? She sounds pretty rude.

LUCY: I guess I got carried away with the excitement of my first really important client. She wants this to be the wedding of the century, and I jumped at the chance to give it to her.

FREDDIE: What are you going to do now?

LUCY: Now that my entire staff has deserted me? I don't know.

FREDDIE: If you could use a helping hand . . .

LUCY: Do you know how to bake a cake?

FREDDIE: Not really.

LUCY: Sew a wedding dress?

FREDDIE: Sorry, I'm all thumbs.

LUCY: Arrange flowers?

FREDDIE: I'd like to, but I've got these allergies. . . .

LUCY: Well, I guess it's the thought that counts. Thanks anyway for offering.

AGNES (*Returning with boxes of invitations*): Here are those invitations, Lucy. I can start—oh, I didn't know you were busy.

LUCY: That's O.K. (*To* FREDDIE) I didn't catch your name.

FREDDIE: Freddie.

LUCY: Freddie, this is my secretary, Agnes.

FREDDIE: Hi, Agnes. (*To* LUCY) And you're—

LUCY: Lucy. Lucy Jackson. Proprietor of the late Hearts and Flowers.

AGNES: Oh, no, did something else happen while I was gone?

LUCY: A mass walk-out. Oh, don't worry—I'm sure they'll be back on Monday morning. It'll just be too late.

AGNES: Look on the bright side, Lucy. I'm still here. The

cake may come out a little lop-sided, and the dress may have a few pins in it, and the flowers may not all match, but somehow, we'll pull this off if we work together—the two of us.

FREDDIE (*Taking off his hat and jacket*): Make that the three of us. Where can I start?

LUCY: But what about your fishing trip?

FREDDIE: Hey—the fish will appreciate the reprieve. (*Takes a box from* AGNES) I can start with the invitations.

LUCY: You're sure you don't mind?

FREDDIE: Of course not! Besides, I owe you something for your map to the lake.

AGNES: I'll go get started. (*Exits*)

LUCY (*To* FREDDIE): And we'll keep our fingers crossed. (*Starts to pick up debris from desk;* FREDDIE *opens a box and suddenly stares.* LUCY *notices him.*) Something wrong, Freddie?

FREDDIE (*Awkwardly*): Uh . . . I'm not sure how to tell you this—(*Phone rings*)

LUCY: Tell me what? Wait—hold that thought, I've got to grab this phone. (*Answers*) Good morning, Hearts and Flowers. This is Miss Jackson. (*Sighs*) Yes, Miss Chippendale? What's that? No, Miss Chippendale. Why, that's terrible. (FREDDIE *starts to move downstage, hands in his pockets.*) Well, did he give any reason? (*Looks up at* FREDDIE) Yes, Miss Chippendale. No, no, Miss Chippendale. I appreciate the call. Yes, well, better luck next time, Miss Chippendale. (*Hangs up, looks at* FREDDIE) That was Miss Chippendale, my client.

FREDDIE (*Not looking at her*): The one who's getting married?

LUCY: Make that *not* getting married. It seems her fiancé had a change of heart.

FREDDIE: Oh?

LUCY: Yes, she says that he suddenly got the urge to borrow a uniform from his chauffeur, throw a fishing pole in the back seat of his limo, and disappear.

FREDDIE: You don't say . . .

LUCY: Freddie?

FREDDIE: Actually, it's Frederick Edward Arlington Simpson the Third. I didn't get a chance to tell you before.

LUCY: And you didn't get a chance to tell Miss Chippendale the wedding is off?

FREDDIE: I haven't seen her for three months, Lucy. I mean, ever since we got engaged, she and her mother have been planning this entire wedding without me. Not once did she ask my opinion.

LUCY: But a wedding is so important to the two people involved. If they really love each other—

FREDDIE: No, I'm afraid Carolyn loves the idea more than she loves me. I wanted a quiet ceremony—she wants the front page. I wanted a few friends—she's inviting half the city. And I wanted a honeymoon someplace peaceful, serene—

LUCY: And with good fishing?

FREDDIE (*Smiling*): Am I that transparent?

LUCY (*Returning the smile*): Like glass.

FREDDIE: This morning she called and said we were honeymooning in Europe. Twenty-seven countries in two weeks. Well, that was the final straw. She was talking so much that I don't think she even heard me hang up the phone.

LUCY: That's too bad.

FREDDIE: I guess it wasn't fair to run out. My chauffeur Harry said it was the thing to do. That's why he gave me one of his uniforms and the keys to the car. But when I saw my name on those invitations and realized all of the trouble you had gone to—

LUCY: Relax, it's O.K. It was turning into a disaster anyway. Miss Chippendale calling to say the whole thing was off is probably the best call I've had from her in months!

FREDDIE: So what are you going to do now?

LUCY: I don't know. The rest of the staff has taken the day off. Maybe I should, too.

FREDDIE: You could always go fishing . . .

LUCY: Gosh, I haven't been fishing in years.

FREDDIE: I've got some extra equipment in the car. If you're not doing anything else—

LUCY (*Excited*): I'd love to! (*Calls off*) Agnes? Listen, the Chippendale wedding is off completely. What do you say we close up the office?

AGNES (*Calling from backstage*): You just made my day!

LUCY (*In satisfaction*): Well, who'd have thought? I guess I was pretty silly to think I had landed the opportunity of a lifetime.

FREDDIE (*Taking her arm*): Oh, but you did, Lucy. (*Escorts her to door*) And, I'm not letting this one get away! (*Curtain*)

THE END

PRODUCTION NOTES

THE WEDDING BELL BLUES

Characters: 2 male, 4 female.

Playing Time: 20 minutes.

Costumes: Lucy, Agnes, Beatrice, and Daphne wear casual clothes. Daphne wears a tape measure around her neck. François wears chef uniform and hat. Freddie wears chauffeur uniform and dark glasses.

Properties: Invitations; boxes; phone; decorations; satin material; flowers; pencil and paper.

Setting: All action takes place in the receptionist area of Hearts and Flowers, a wedding service. Sign on wall reads, YOU GET THE GROOM . . . AND WE DO THE REST. The color scheme is pink and white, festooned with hearts, bells, cherubs, etc. Agnes's desk is center; entry door to office is right, hallway to adjoining offices is left.

Lighting and Sound: No special lighting effects. Sounds of phone ringing.

Author! Author!

Characters

LARRY LITERARY, *talk show host*
ALICE STEVENSON, *travel writer*
R. R. HOOD, *romance novelist*
SNOW CHARMING, *gourmet cookbook author*

TIME: *The present.*
SETTING: *Hollywood studio set. A desk is center; three comfortable chairs are left of desk. Sign reading* ON THE AIR *hangs from ceiling above stage. Exit is up left.*
AT RISE: *Stage is dark.* LARRY LITERARY *is sitting at desk. With a musical flourish from live band or recording, lights come up and* LARRY *waves to audience.*
LARRY: Good evening, ladies and gentlemen. I'm your host, Larry Literary, welcoming you to another hour of every reader's favorite show, Bibliophile's Babble, the program that takes you beyond the cover, behind the printed page, and straight to the heart of the typewriter—the authors themselves! And what a lineup we've got tonight, folks! Just back from a whirlwind tour is highly acclaimed travel writer Alice Stevenson, with helpful tips on how to navigate down rabbit holes, communicate with royalty, and what foods to stay away from while on the road. And I know you won't want to switch channels when I tell you

that Bibliophile's Babble scored a major victory over the
other networks in this first-of-a-lifetime event—an inter-
view with the undisputed leader of Gothic romances, the
elusive R. R. Hood. She'll be sharing a few excerpts from
her latest book, but don't rush to the bookstore for it just
yet—if you do, you'll miss the grand finale. Snow Charming, gourmet cookbook author, has something of interest
for our viewers on a budget—her new bestseller, *Cooking
for Seven or More*. (*Looks at watch*) Gosh! The time is
flying already. Join me now in welcoming our first guest,
Ms. Alice Stevenson! (*Fanfare and applause as* ALICE
STEVENSON *enters. She has long blond hair, wears ruffled blue dress, knee socks, and black patent leather shoes.
She also wears dark glasses, carries backpack containing
book, and has a pair of tennis shoes tied together by their
laces and slung over her shoulder. She shakes hands with*
LARRY *and takes a seat.*) Welcome to Bibliophile's Babble, Alice.

ALICE (*Taking off glasses*): Thank you, Larry. It's great to
be back in—excuse me, but where are we again?

LARRY: Hollywood.

ALICE: Ah, yes. Hollywood. Sorry. I travel so much, I
sometimes have trouble remembering where I am.

LARRY: I hope you remembered to bring your new book,
Curiouser, Curiouser.

ALICE (*Taking copy of book out of backpack and handing
it to* LARRY): Right here, Larry.

LARRY: Peculiar title, isn't it?

ALICE: Oh, on the contrary. Travel these days can be quite
a curious muddle if you don't know what you're doing.

LARRY: And your new book clears that up?

ALICE: Clear as a looking glass.

LARRY: Mind telling us about it?

ALICE: Well, it has pictures by the hundreds. Pictures by
the thousands. I just adore pictures.

LARRY: Didn't the reviews say that this story takes place in a rabbit hole?

ALICE: And that's the truth, Larry! What a trip that was! Which reminds me of my first tip for travelers: Always leave a trail when wandering about in foreign lands, or you'll never find your way back!

LARRY: But what about the locals? Weren't they helpful in giving directions?

ALICE: Oh, I'm sure they meant well, though at times they seemed quite determined to confuse me. And speaking of confusion, never buy clothes when abroad.

LARRY: Why is that?

ALICE: Well, just from personal experience, Larry, I find that my size fluctuates dramatically when I'm away from home. That was particularly true on my last adventure.

LARRY: But don't you think foreign food has something to do with that? People's eating habits do change when they're on vacation . . . or so I've read.

ALICE: That's why I've decided from now on to start carrying my own food. (*Pats her backpack*) In my pack, for instance, I have ham and cheese croissants, crab pâté, grapes, kiwis, chocolate eclairs, diet soda, and half a turkey. Of course, taste preferences do vary from traveler to traveler. It's much safer to take foods you're used to rather than taking a chance on items labeled "Drink Me" or "Eat Me." Other countries just aren't as careful these days about additives and preservatives as we are here.

LARRY: Just one more question before I bring on our next guest, Alice.

ALICE: Certainly.

LARRY: I understand that you plan to do some investigative reporting on future trips.

ALICE: That's right, Larry. In fact, after the show tonight, I'm catching a plane with Renaldo Riviera to cover two major exposés in Europe.

LARRY: Can you give us a hint?

ALICE: Well, our first stop is a toy workshop run by a man who claims he can turn wooden marionettes into real people.

LARRY: Sounds suspicious to me. What's the other one?

ALICE: That will be live network coverage showing Renaldo and me opening the secret safe of a man who for years has been turning straw into gold.

LARRY: And you think the safe contains his gold treasure?

ALICE: What we're really hoping for is his birth certificate. We've been promised half a kingdom if we can learn his name.

LARRY: Well, your secret's safe with me, Alice. And speaking of secrets, our next guest is every bit as mysterious as the Gothic tales she turns out year after year. A recluse by nature, she has finally consented to make her very first public appearance on our program. Welcome her now, Ms. R.R. Hood. (*Applause as* R.R. HOOD, *wearing full-length hooded cape and carrying book, enters.* R.R. *shakes hands with* LARRY, *then dramatically removes cape, revealing identity as man, not woman.* LARRY *gasps.*) You're not R. R. Hood! What have you done with her?

R. R.: Perhaps I should introduce myself. I am Robert Rubin Hood.

LARRY: Oh, you must be R.R. Hood's brother, right? I hope R. R. isn't sick.

R. R.: Never felt better, thanks.

LARRY (*Shocked*): You don't mean you're —

R.R.: R.R. Hood. It's short for Robert Rubin.

ALICE: And to think, all these years I thought you were a woman!

R.R.: So you've read my books?

ALICE: I never leave home without them.

R.R.: Great! You'll have a new one to add to your collection. (*Displays book*) I call it *Stranger in the Forest*.

LARRY: What's this one about?

R.R.: Well, the book's about a young woman named Maisie who disregards her family's warnings and gets involved with someone she meets on the way to her grandmother's.

ALICE: Who is he?

R.R.: Howard DeWulff. His family comes from the wrong side of the tracks, you see. By day, Howard's a dance instructor. Fox trots, that sort of thing. But at night . . .

LARRY: Yes?

R.R.: He runs with a bloodthirsty pack in the woods and is an absolute animal.

ALICE: So what does Maisie see in him?

R.R.: For her, it's puppy love. She thinks they have a future together. And since she's a dancer, too, she thinks they can be the next Fred and Ginger. Her mother tells Howard to keep his paws off Maisie, but Maisie truly believes that music can soothe the savage beast.

LARRY: Do you mind reading us a sentence or two?

R.R.: I'd be delighted. (*Crosses center and opens book*) I'll read the first sentence to set the scene. (*Clears throat and reads*) "'Howard DeWulff is no good,' her mother told her, but Maisie, in her youthful innocence, knew her mother was wrong, for she remembered the way her heart skipped a beat the first time she saw him emerge from the forest, toss his fedora on the street light and tap dance his way to the corner, his eyes just then meeting hers, the gleam of animal magnetism bright and alive and telling her, without words, that her days behind the perfume counter at the five and dime were numbered and that they'd soon be a team that dance critics would talk about in admiration over cherry chocolates and cappuccino and that her family, stubborn as they were, would come to love him as much as she did."

ALICE (*Mesmerized*): Wow! I'm hooked already, and that was only the first page.

R.R.: Actually, it was only the first sentence. Would you like to hear more?

LARRY: We'll have to take a raincheck, R.R. Our next guest has a mouthwatering surprise that just won't wait. (R.R. *takes seat next to* ALICE.)

ALICE: Who is it, Larry?

LARRY: Well, in the past five years, her life has truly come full circle. The target of a vindictive queen, and presumed dead, this young princess was in fact rescued by a band of miners in the woods who offered to let her live in their house in exchange for light housework.

R.R. (*Taking out notebook and pencil*): That's incredible. Do you think she'd mind if I used that plot in my next book?

LARRY: Well, I don't know, R.R., but pay attention, because the plot thickens. Just last week, she married Prince Charming and regained her royal title. But this good fortune hasn't gone to her head. Concerned about the plight of poor peasants, she has just brought out an exciting cookbook compiled from her years with the dwarfs. Let's have a big hand for our next author, Snow Charming. (*Applause as* SNOW CHARMING *enters, in traditional costume and page boy hairstyle. She carries sack of groceries and eagerly shakes hands with others.*) Welcome to the show, Mrs. Charming.

SNOW: Please call me Snow. And I'm so excited to be here!

LARRY: Congratulations are in order, too, I hear.

SNOW (*Exuberantly*): Oh, yes. I'm going to have my own cooking program!

R.R.: Tell us about it, Snow!

SNOW: Well, in addition to my own cooking demonstrations each week, I'm going to feature a special guest who will talk about a food-related issue.

LARRY: Do you mind letting our viewers in on the opening line-up?

SNOW: Not at all, Larry. The first week, we've invited Mrs. Sprat. She's going to be talking about the issue of fat vs. lean, along with her husband, Jack.

ALICE: It sounds exciting.

SNOW: We'll also hear from Mrs. Pumpkin Eater. She's written a new book called *Breaking Out of Your Shell*.

LARRY: Yes, as a matter of fact, she'll be appearing on *our* program, too, in a few weeks.

ALICE: Anyone else?

SNOW: Well, my agent has just closed a deal with Mrs. Hubbard. She's put together an especially interesting lecture on how to make do with nothing.

R.R.: My goodness, Snow, you've certainly come a long way.

SNOW: Yes, I suppose I have. I have the dwarfs to thank for that. They were very helpful while I was gathering material for the book.

R.R.: Tell us what it's like to be married to the Prince!

SNOW: Oh, he's very nice to me. He's taking singing lessons now, you know.

ALICE: Does he help out in the kitchen?

SNOW: Certainly. I wouldn't have it any other way.

R.R. (*Pointing*): What's in the bag?

SNOW: Well, I've brought each of you a copy of the new book. They're autographed, too. (*Hands out books. Others ad lib appreciation.*)

R.R. (*Looking through book*): This chapter on brussels sprouts looks interesting.

SNOW: Yes, I use them a lot in making meals stretch. When your guests don't go back for seconds, you have more leftovers and, thus, more meal possibilities the rest of the week.

LARRY (*Leafing through book*): I see that you also get into foreign foods in chapter seven.

SNOW: Yes, Larry, all your friends will think you went to French cooking school. Actually, the secret is to add French words to whatever you serve. For instance, *Le* Cheeseburger . . . or Soup Suzette . . . or my personal favorite, Okra Au Revoir. Everything in the chapter is cheap to prepare—it only *sounds* expensive.

R.R.: A very worthwhile tip, Snow.

SNOW: You can also add intrigue to an otherwise bland meal by making it sound exotic. For instance, Carrot Surprise . . . Tropical Tofu . . . Sinful Tripe. . . . Spinach Supreme. Take my word for it, the dwarfs never missed a meal.

ALICE: How do you feel about the new interest in "natural" foods?

SNOW: Oh, I think they're very beneficial. As a matter of fact, (*Rummages in bag*) I just happen to have something here that's as natural as can be. (*Pulls out apples, passes them around*)

R.R.: Ooh! Apples!

LARRY: Snow, you shouldn't have!

ALICE: They look delicious! And perfect for my next trip!

LARRY: Where on earth did you get such shiny, red apples?

SNOW: It was quite unusual, actually. A woman was peddling them door to door. They looked so tasty, I just couldn't resist. (*Raising her apple as if in toast*) Well, everyone, enjoy! (*Everyone but SNOW bites into their apples at the same time; SNOW suddenly looks confused and muses, her back to others.*) Hmm. I just remembered something. (*Others are suddenly reacting to poison, holding throats, slumping over, etc. SNOW doesn't see them.*) That woman who came to the door. Where have I seen her before? She looked familiar, but I just can't place her. (*One by one, ALICE, LARRY, and R.R. collapse.*) She was awfully nice, of course, insisting that I take as many apples as I wanted and encouraging me to eat them right away.

I'll have to mention it to the Prince tonight, although I'm sure it's nothing to worry about. (*Starts to turn upstage*) Anyway, as I was saying . . . (*Suddenly notices others, turns to audience, puzzled, then shrugs*) Oh well, it must have been something they ate. (*Bites into her own apple and there is immediate blackout. Curtain*)

THE END

PRODUCTION NOTES

AUTHOR! AUTHOR!

Characters: 2 female; 2 male.
Playing Time: 15 minutes.
Costumes: Contemporary dress for Larry and R.R. (R.R. also wears full-length hooded cape upon first entrance); Alice wears ruffled blue dress, knee socks, black patent shoes. She also has long blond hair and wears dark glasses. Snow Charming wears traditional costume.
Properties: Backpack; books; tennis shoes; bag of groceries; apples.
Lighting: Blackout at end.
Sound: Music, as indicated in text.

For round-the-table reading . . .

The Magic Mermaid

Characters

FOUR STORYTELLERS
FISHERMAN
ANGELINA, *Fisherman's sister*
FISHERMAN'S NEPHEW
FISHERMAN'S NIECE
MERMAID

TIME: *Many, many years ago.*
SETTING: *The shores off southern England.*
1ST STORYTELLER:
  On the shores of Southern England
  where the wind blows ever cold,
  They tell a tale of fishermen
  with strength and courage bold.
2ND STORYTELLER:
  Each morning on the Cornwall tide
  they'd leave their village shore,
  and trade the sweet tranquility
  to face the ocean's roar.
3RD STORYTELLER:
  They'd fill their nets and load their decks
  with fish both large and small.

But when the sea was selfish,
they brought nothing home at all.
4TH STORYTELLER:
A season such as this had come;
the winter had set in.
A time of darkness spelling doom.
Our story shall begin.
1ST STORYTELLER:
Our hero's name is William,
a fisherman by trade.
2ND STORYTELLER:
His sister's Angelina,
a pretty Cornish maid.
FISHERMAN:
I'm off, dear sister, wish me well
and help me with my coat.
ANGELINA (*Concerned*):
Oh, William, please, be sensible,
and don't go to your boat.
The wind is howling like a wolf.
The sea is almost black!
FISHERMAN:
Oh, Angelina, don't despair:
I promise I'll be back.
ANGELINA:
A storm is coming, William.
And I fear a bad one, too.
Come lay a cozy fire instead
and have some carrot stew.
FISHERMAN:
Dear Angelina, sweet and kind,
I promise I'll take care.
ANGELINA: But must you go?
FISHERMAN:
You know I must.
Our cupboards are quite bare.

The sea's our sole survival.
It gives us fish to sell,
and when we show her our respect,
in turn, she treats us well.
NEPHEW:
May I go with you, Uncle?
For you said someday I might.
FISHERMAN:
Some day, it's true, I said so, lad.
Yes, when the time is right.
NEPHEW:
What's wrong with going out today?
My arms are young and strong.
FISHERMAN:
Perhaps next week, we'll wait and see.
Besides, I won't be long.
NIECE:
I brought your favorite scarf to wear
and gloves to warm you, too.
FISHERMAN:
A lucky man I am, dear child,
to have a niece like you!
ANGELINA:
Please don't go out to sea today—
such angry waves await!
FISHERMAN:
The ocean is our friend, you know.
I'm off, I'm running late.
1ST STORYTELLER:
So out the door our hero went,
despite her fervent plea,
and strode down to the windswept docks
and looked out at the sea.
FISHERMAN:
A lucky day, a journey safe!

2ND STORYTELLER:
  A prayer he said out loud.
3RD STORYTELLER:
  Then rowed his boat into the bay
  through turbulence and cloud.
ANGELINA (*Anxiously*):
  I never should have let him go.
  I fear the very worst.
4TH STORYTELLER:
  Just as she spoke the heavens split
  And clouds began to burst.
1ST STORYTELLER:
  The thunder roared across the sky
  and lightning shone in gold.
2ND STORYTELLER:
  While out at sea, the waves grew high
  and winds blew deadly cold.
FISHERMAN (*Calling fearfully*): Protect me!
3RD STORYTELLER:
  The man cried out
  and clung to every hope,
  as sails were shredded by the wind
  and tangled in the rope.
4TH STORYTELLER:
  But just as all his strength gave out,
  his eyes beheld a shore.
1ST STORYTELLER:
  And promised him a refuge
  till calm returned once more.
2ND STORYTELLER:
  No sooner had he felt the earth
  beneath his callused hand
  than he heard a mournful whimper
  from across the rocky sand.

FISHERMAN (*Alarmed*):
  A woman's cry, I swear it,
  yet I see no one in sight.
3RD STORYTELLER:
  And he squinted in frustration
  that his eyes might pierce the night.
FISHERMAN:
  But wait, beyond's a movement
  and her cries are growing clear.
4TH STORYTELLER:
  So he crawled in their direction
  and the crying brought him near.
1ST STORYTELLER:
  A face as fair as angels'
  and curls as black as night.
  Our hero gasped in wonder
  at so beautiful a sight.
2ND STORYTELLER:
  A web of green enwrapped her
  in seaweed to her waist,
  and our hero sought to free her
  with efficiency and haste.
3RD STORYTELLER:
  But as he pulled her from the weeds
  amazement filled his eyes,
  for never had he seen before
  so shocking a surprise.
FISHERMAN (*In disbelief*):
  It can't be true . . . or can it?
  It's a dream, a sailor's wish,
  to behold a maid half-human
  and the other half a fish!
MERMAID: Please free me, sir!
4TH STORYTELLER:
  The mermaid begged.

MERMAID:
　I'll die if left ashore.
　I need to feel the sea's caress
　and breathe her cold once more.
FISHERMAN:
　But if I take you back to town,
　the crowds that we could fetch!
　For none have seen a mermaid girl.
　You'd make a novel catch!
1ST STORYTELLER:
　A smile then spread across her lips,
　as the fisherman drew near.
MERMAID:
　Release me, sir, and you shall have
　the wish you hold most dear.
FISHERMAN:
　Only one? A single wish?
　That's difficult for me.
　Perhaps you'd bend the rules a bit
　and grant me two or three?
MERMAID:
　Three it is, then, but be wise
　and choose them all with care
　for wishes wished in recklessness
　bring nothing but despair.
4TH STORYTELLER:
　A puzzle, thought the fisherman,
　for many needs had he.
　So many things they'd gone without
　in living off the sea.
　His widowed sister's clothes were old.
　Their house was prone to leak.
　His niece and nephew needed school
　or faced a future bleak.

FISHERMAN (*Excitedly*):
A grander house would serve us well,
and a larger boat to fish,
and all the gold my arms can hold,
and food on every dish!

MERMAID:
If those are things that bring you joy
and refuge from the past
then wish them now and throw me back
before I breathe my last.

1ST STORYTELLER:
But in that moment, grave and still,
he had a change of mind,
and knew the things he asked for
were not generous or kind.
His village was a poor one;
the winters took their due,
and sickness paid a visit
to every house he knew.

4TH STORYTELLER:
His own kin had been luckier
in keeping up their health.
In this he saw blessing
far more valuable than wealth.

MERMAID:
The silence has your tongue, dear sir.
Your wishes I await.

2ND STORYTELLER:
And in her words he saw a way
to change the hand of fate.
For mortal gifts could not replace
the passing of a friend
or dry the tears of children
left orphaned in the end.

FISHERMAN:

I've given careful thought to this,
and I wish for special skills
to help my fellow villagers
live long and cure their ills.

MERMAID:

It's done, sir, you shall have the gift
to heal the weak and sick.
My ears await your next request,
but please, sir, make it quick.

FISHERMAN:

The second wish, my pretty one—
if your magic can hold fast—
I want my gift of healing
to be something that will last.
With every generation
of those who bear our name,
grant them this charm of healing,
let their powers be the same.

3RD STORYTELLER:

The mermaid gave a nod of yes
and bade him say the third.

4TH STORYTELLER:

The wind blew loud, a thunderous roar
His voice was barely heard.

MERMAID:

What's that again, sir?
Make your wish, then quickly set me free,
for time is of the essence.
I'll die outside the sea.

FISHERMAN:

My third one is a selfish wish,
a foolish wish to make.
But I know if I release you,

then my heart will surely break.
I'll let you go back to the sea,
but I ask you in its place
that our farewell not be final
and I once more see your face.
Promise you'll return one day
when years have made me gray,
and take me to your ocean's depths
and there I'll always stay.
MERMAID:
   I swear I'll keep that promise, sir,
   and keep the other two.
   Now, take me to the water's edge
   that I might swim from you.
1ST STORYTELLER:
   And so he set the mermaid loose
   and watched her swim to sea—
   and wondered if she'd keep her word
   and grant his wishes three.
2ND STORYTELLER:
   Very soon, though, did he find
   her spell had taken hold
   for he had the gift of healing,
   a gift more fine than gold.
3RD STORYTELLER:
   His reputation blossomed.
   His name spread far and wide—
   and all thanks to a mermaid
   who, without him, would have died.
4TH STORYTELLER:
   And though the years had aged him
   and he ne'er more went to sail,
   he often thought about her
   when the weather turned to gale.

1ST STORYTELLER:
 So on a winter evening
 while the town lay fast asleep,
 he rowed out past the harbor
 to the waters cold and deep.
FISHERMAN:
 My hands have done their healing
 and that gift has thus been passed.
 So now I ask you, mermaid,
 that you grant to me the last.
MERMAID:
 Just take my hand and come with me.
3RD STORYTELLER:
 She whispered on the wind.
4TH STORYTELLER:
 And from that night, the fisherman
 was never seen again.

THE END

Secret Agents in Disguise

Characters

JACK PHOENIX } *secret agents*
CLAIRE WATERS }
BARBARA TURNER
MYRNA, *her jet-setting friend*
MOTHER, *Barbara's mother*
PRINCE BABBALONEY, *government witness*
OTIS, *Prince's aide*
NIGHTSHADE, *sinister secret agent*

SCENE 1

TIME: *The present.*

SETTING: *Produce section of grocery store. At center is counter with fresh fruit. Upstage and on either side are display racks of grocery items.*

AT RISE: JACK PHOENIX *is downstage of display counter, holding banana as if it's a telephone and talking into it. He wears trench coat and white fedora, and is looking about anxiously.*

JACK: But there *has* to be a place, Chief! The congressional hearing isn't until ten tomorrow. . . . I know, I know. (*Checks watch*) I'll pick them up at the airport . . . . Uh-huh. . . . Well, Claire's supposed to be here any minute.

Maybe she'll have an idea. (CLAIRE, *wearing trench coat, white fedora, and dark glasses enters right, pushing a full shopping cart.*) I know, Chief. The fate of the country could hinge on this one. (*Notices* CLAIRE) Gotta go, Chief. Phoenix out. ("*Hangs up" banana by putting it back with other bunches in display*) Bad news, Claire. (*They stand back to back.*)

CLAIRE (*Talking to* JACK *over her shoulder*): What is it, Phoenix?

JACK: The Chief says Prince Babbaloney and his aide got an early flight. I'm meeting them in half an hour.

CLAIRE: But the hearing's not until tomorrow morning.

JACK: Right. So we have to hide them until then.

CLAIRE: How about the record shop?

JACK (*Shaking head*): No good. Nightshade's already got a couple of agents staking it out.

CLAIRE: The dry cleaners?

JACK: Nope. It's clear across town. If Nightshade plans a hit, there's no way we could protect the Prince and his aide. We need someplace small, someplace different, a spot Nightshade would never consider.

CLAIRE: Do you really think she's going to leave a single stone in Washington unturned? If Prince Babbaloney goes on the stand tomorrow, he'll blow the lid off her entire South American operation.

JACK: Right. We've got to think of something. (BARBARA TURNER *and* MYRNA *enter left, with shopping carts.* MYRNA *wears a "punk" outfit.* BARBARA *is conservatively dressed.*)

CLAIRE: Uh-oh. (JACK *starts to turn.*) Don't look.

JACK: What's wrong?

CLAIRE: Civilians.

JACK: Act natural. (CLAIRE *pretends to study shopping list.* JACK *puts his hands in his pockets and whistles casu-*

ally; the two of them remain standing back to back, eaves-dropping on the following conversation.)

MYRNA: And then we're catching the midnight Concorde to Rio! (*Giggles*) I can hardly catch my breath just thinking about it!

BARBARA: Sounds wonderful.

MYRNA: Why don't you come along? There's plenty of room.

BARBARA: You're joking.

MYRNA: No—it'll be fun. You don't get out enough, Barbara. You really don't.

BARBARA (*Defensively*): Sure I do.

MYRNA: Going to the office, then going home is hardly "going out." How do you ever expect to meet anyone?

BARBARA: Oh, when the time is right, my ship will come in.

MYRNA: Yes, and you'll be too busy at your computer screen to notice it.

BARBARA: Thanks for the invitation, Myrna, but—

MYRNA: But what?

BARBARA (*Shrugging*): I guess I just like the quiet things. A quiet house, a quiet neighborhood . . .

MYRNA (*Laughing*): So quiet I'll bet they roll up the streets at night! (JACK *snaps his fingers and nudges* CLAIRE.)

JACK: Claire! I've got a great idea. Come here. (*He goes upstage of counter;* CLAIRE *follows him. They duck down behind counter.*)

MYRNA: What do you say we go to a movie tonight? Or how about that new dance club on M Street?

BARBARA: Well . . .

MYRNA: I'll pick you up at seven.

BARBARA: Myrna!

MYRNA (*Ignoring* BARBARA's *protests*): See you! (*Exits with cart;* BARBARA *sighs heavily, looks over produce items.*)

CLAIRE (*Standing up from behind counter*): That's the most ridiculous thing I've ever heard!

JACK: No, it isn't—it's perfect!

CLAIRE: The Chief will never agree to it.

JACK: All he asked was that I find a place. (*Checks watch*) I'll take care of the details. Why don't you go pick up the Prince and his aide. As soon as I get the address, I'll be in touch.

CLAIRE: Are you sure you know what you're doing?

JACK: No . . . but it's the only chance we've got right now. (CLAIRE *exits.* JACK *approaches* BARBARA, *who is putting a bunch of bananas in her cart.*) Excuse me, miss. I wonder if you would help me?

BARBARA: I can try.

JACK (*Looking around, then speaking confidentially*): I'm looking for a place to hide something.

BARBARA: I beg your pardon?

JACK: It's vital to national security.

BARBARA: You want to hide something vital to national security in a grocery store?

JACK: Not some*thing.* Some*one.* And not here. Somewhere else.

BARBARA: I don't understand.

JACK (*Pulling out wallet, opening it, flashing badge*): Maybe this will explain it.

BARBARA (*Starting to read*): Criminal Federation of— (JACK *puts wallet away before she can finish.*)

JACK: The name of the agency I work for isn't really important. But getting an important witness on the stand is. Would you be willing to help us?

BARBARA: Me? What could *I* possibly do?

JACK: If I tell you, you're absolutely sworn to secrecy.

BARBARA: But I don't even know your name.

JACK: Then we're even—I don't know yours either.

BARBARA: Barbara Turner.

JACK (*Shaking hands*): Jack Phoenix. Now, here's the plan.

(*Sound of phone ringing is coming from bananas in* BAR-
BARA's *cart. Puzzled,* BARBARA *looks down at her
cart.*)

BARBARA: Did you hear that?

JACK: Hear what? (*Phone rings.*)

BARBARA: That. (*Leans forward*) It sounded as if it was
coming from my shopping cart.

JACK (*Putting hand out*): Uh—allow me. (*Picks up banana,
speaks into it.* BARBARA *watches, stunned.*) Yeah, Chief?
. . . It's under control. . . . No, I'd better explain later.
We're not really going by the book on this one . . . O.K.
Phoenix out. (*Puts banana back into cart*)

BARBARA: What was that all about?

JACK: Come on, I'll explain while we're walking. (*They exit
right as curtain closes.*)

* * * * *

SCENE 2

BEFORE RISE: BARBARA *and* JACK *walk slowly from
stage right to left.* BARBARA *carries two small bags of
groceries.*

BARBARA: Why can't you just put him up in a hotel for the
night? Or buy him a disguise?

JACK: Because it wouldn't be safe. Nightshade is absolutely
deadly, Barbara. The Prince's testimony is crucial and
Nightshade knows it.

BARBARA: But we just live in an ordinary house, hardly
the sort of place one can hide royalty.

JACK: Did you say "we"?

BARBARA: Yes, my mother lives there, too. But don't
worry—she's playing bridge at a friend's tonight, and she's
going to exercise class first thing in the morning. With any

luck, she'll never notice the Prince and—what did you say his valet's name was? (*They stop center.*)

JACK: Otis.

BARBARA: Right. Anyway, Mother won't notice a thing. She's a bit—uh—flaky.

JACK: Let's hope for the best.

BARBARA (*Skeptically*): I'm still not sure about this, Jack.

JACK: What's wrong?

BARBARA: Well, as I said, I've never had royalty in the house before. What do I do? What do I say? And what about servants? We don't have any.

JACK: Just be yourself. The Prince's safety is what's important now. Servants and protocol and that stuff don't matter.

BARBARA: Well, if you say so.

JACK (*With a smile*): That's the spirit! (*Their eyes meet for a moment; flustered, JACK breaks the silence by pointing left.*) That's your house?

BARBARA: Yes, I'll show you around before Claire gets here with the Prince. (*They exit left as curtain opens.*)

* * * * *

SETTING: *Barbara's living room. Center is sofa, coffee table with phone, and armchairs. At left is front door. Exit upstage leads to rest of house; exit right, to kitchen.*

AT RISE: JACK *and* BARBARA *enter left.*

JACK (*Pleased*): Oh, Barbara, this'll be perfect. Mind if I look around?

BARBARA: Not at all. (*Points upstage*) The spare room is down the hall on the left. (*He exits as BARBARA proceeds right with bags of groceries. MOTHER, a fluttery type, enters right, stirring mixture in bowl.*)

MOTHER: Hi, dear. Have a good day at work?

BARBARA (*Taken aback*): Mother! What are you doing here?

MOTHER (*Shrugging*): I live here.

BARBARA: I mean, what are you doing here now? I thought you were playing bridge tonight.

MOTHER: Oh, we're still on for bridge. I wouldn't miss it for anything.

BARBARA (*With a sigh of relief*): That's good. (*Continues right*)

MOTHER: But we're having it here instead. That's why I'm baking a cake. (BARBARA *stops short.*)

BARBARA: What?!

MOTHER: Which reminds me, dear, would you like to be our fourth? Lorraine's sick—that's why we had to move the game over here.

BARBARA (*Flustered*): Uh—actually, I sort of had plans tonight, and—(JACK *reenters upstage, startled to see* MOTHER.)

MOTHER: Oh, I didn't realize you had a guest, dear.

BARBARA (*Quickly*): This is a friend from work.

MOTHER: Hi. I'm Doris Turner, Barbara's mother.

JACK: Nice to meet you. (*Looks nervously at watch*)

MOTHER (*In questioning tone*): And you're—

JACK (*Quickly*): Running late. (*Starts left*) Listen, Barbara, thanks for your help on that (*With emphasis*) project.

BARBARA: But what if I need *help* with it? What if I run into *problems*? You know . . . unexpectedly?

JACK: I'll be in touch. Don't worry. (*Starts to exit*)

MOTHER: Aren't you going with him, Barbara?

BARBARA: No, Mother.

MOTHER: I thought you said you had plans tonight.

BARBARA (*Quickly*): Right. Um—plans to work on something here. Yes—here by myself. I have a project due Monday, first thing.

MOTHER: Well, if you ask me, Barbara, you should take a break now and then. Get out and do things. That's what weekends are for. (*Sound of phone ringing is heard in* BARBARA's *grocery bag.*) Just a minute—let me get that. (*Starts for phone on coffee table. Phone in bag rings again.* JACK *and* BARBARA *exchange glances, and* MOTHER *stops, puzzled.*)

JACK (*Crossing quickly to* BARBARA): That's probably for me. (*Takes bag*)

MOTHER: *What's* for you?

JACK: This bag. (*Crossing right*) You wanted this in the kitchen, didn't you? (*Exits*)

MOTHER: What a nice young man, Barbara! What did you say he does?

BARBARA (*Uncomfortably*): I don't think I did.

MOTHER: You said he was a friend from work.

BARBARA: Yes . . . uh . . . Accounting. He's from Accounting.

MOTHER: That must be why he's so conscientious. So what project are you working on?

BARBARA: Well, it's—um . . . (*Doorbell rings.*) The doorbell! I'll get it! (*Crossing left*)

MOTHER: I'll just go help your friend in the kitchen. (*Starts right*)

BARBARA: Wait! (MOTHER *stops.*) Don't you want to see who's at the door?

MOTHER (*Puzzled*): I thought *you* were going to get it.

BARBARA: But it might be for you.

MOTHER (*Handing* BARBARA *mixing bowl as she crosses left*): You're acting awfully strange, dear. (*Opens door to* CLAIRE, OTIS, *who wears suit, and* PRINCE, *in African garb.*)

CLAIRE (*To* MOTHER): Are you Barbara Turner?

MOTHER: No, I'm her mother. (*Gestures to* BARBARA)

This is Barbara. (BARBARA *hands bowl back to* MOTHER.)

CLAIRE: I believe you were expecting us?

BARBARA (*Flustered*): Yes, of course. Come on in. Make yourselves at home. (MOTHER *looks from* CLAIRE *to* PRINCE *to* OTIS, *completely puzzled*.) Just a few friends from the office, Mother.

MOTHER (*To* CLAIRE, PRINCE, OTIS): Oh—so you're working on that project with Barbara. (*They look at her confused*.)

BARBARA: Actually—

JACK (*Reentering*): Oh, good! You're here. (*To* CLAIRE) Any problems?

CLAIRE: None so far. (PRINCE *wanders off upstage into hallway*.)

MOTHER (*Alarmed*): Where's he going?

OTIS: Oh, don't mind him. He just wants to get the lay of the land.

MOTHER: I see. So, are you in Accounting, too?

OTIS: I beg your pardon?

MOTHER: Barbara's father was an accountant, you know.

BARBARA (*Quickly taking* MOTHER's *arm; urgently*): Mother, may I see you in the kitchen a minute? (*They start right*. MOTHER *exits first;* BARBARA *steps back to apologize to others*.) Jack, I feel terrible. Everything's going all wrong!

JACK: Maybe not. (*Pause*) Your mother thinks we all work together, right? That we're working overtime?

BARBARA: It was all I could come up with. (*To* OTIS) I hope you and the Prince aren't offended.

OTIS (*With a smile*): Please, Miss Turner. No apology is required. You're doing us a great service on such short notice.

MOTHER (*Reentering*): Barbara, I thought you said you wanted to talk to me about something.

JACK (*Looking at watch*): Gosh, look at the time! We'd better get back to the office, Claire. (*They start left.*)

MOTHER (*To* OTIS): Aren't you going with them?

BARBARA (*Trying to explain*): Uh—he and the other guy are staying for a while, Mother. We're sort of working on something . . . for the office.

MOTHER: I thought you said you were working alone.

BARBARA: Well—(PRINCE *reenters and wanders off right.*)

JACK (*As he and* CLAIRE *exit*): We'll be in touch.

OTIS: What your daughter is trying to say, Mrs. Turner, is that the project is confidential.

MOTHER: Oh, well why didn't you say that in the first place? I'll just leave you two alone to work on whatever it is you're working on. (*Exits right*)

BARBARA (*To* OTIS): Thanks for helping me out like that.

OTIS: On the contrary, Miss Turner. You're the one helping us. And now, if you don't mind, I'd like to go over some notes for the hearing tomorrow.

BARBARA (*Pointing upstage*): There's a study down the hall to your left.

OTIS: Thank you. (*Exits upstage*)

MOTHER (*Reentering right*): Barbara, when the bridge club gets here, just send them around back. That way we won't disturb you and—(*Suddenly*) Where did he go?

BARBARA: He's in the study.

MOTHER: I see. Well, I hope you don't mind, but I put the big silent one to work frosting my cake.

BARBARA: You *what?*

MOTHER (*Nonchalantly*): Well, he was just standing around with nothing to do.

BARBARA (*Horrified*): Mother, you can't ask him to— (*Doorbell rings.*)

MOTHER: Goodness! More friends of yours, Barbara?

BARBARA (*Dryly*): I never knew I had so many. (*Crosses to door; opens it to* CLAIRE *who wears black fedora*) Claire!

MOTHER: I'll be in the kitchen if you need me, dear. (*Exits right*)

BARBARA (*As* CLAIRE *enters*): Is something wrong? Where's Jack?

CLAIRE: Oh, I dropped him off at headquarters. (*Hands* BARBARA *small bag*) And then I picked this up for you.

BARBARA (*Looking into bag*): Chinese food?

CLAIRE: I didn't want you to have to go to any extra trouble for the Prince.

BARBARA: That's really nice, Claire. Why don't you join us? It looks as if you brought plenty.

CLAIRE: No, no. I've got to be running along. There are lots of security details we still have to work out for tomorrow. See you! (*Exits.* BARBARA *closes door and starts walking left. After a few moments, doorbell rings again; puzzled, she goes back, opens it to* JACK.)

BARBARA (*Surprised*): Jack! What are you doing here?

JACK (*Entering*): I came back to apologize for putting you on the spot with your mother. You're terrific to be putting up with all this. (BARBARA *closes door.*)

BARBARA: Oh, it's nothing.

JACK (*Indicating bag*): What's in the bag?

BARBARA: Chinese food. Claire just brought it by.

JACK (*Puzzled*): Claire? But that's impossible. I just dropped her off at headquarters.

BARBARA: I don't get it. She said she dropped you off.

JACK: Oh, no!

BARBARA: Jack—what is it? (JACK *grabs bag, throws open door, tosses bag out, then pulls* BARBARA *to the floor.*)

JACK: Get down! (*Offstage, loud explosion is heard.*) Are you O.K.?

BARBARA: Yes, I'm fine. But what's going on?

JACK: I don't think that was Claire you just saw.

BARBARA: But it looked just like her. (*Pause*) You know, there was something a little bit different about her, but I just can't put my finger on it.

CLAIRE (*Entering left, holding out a gun*): Maybe it was the hat. (*Front door remains open.*)

BARBARA: Claire!

JACK: Nightshade!

BARBARA: Nightshade?

JACK: I forgot to tell you she's a master of disguise. (*To* NIGHTSHADE) What did you do with Claire?

NIGHTSHADE: Oh, she's fine, although I'm afraid she's too tied up to help you. (*Looks around*) Where is he?

BARBARA (*Innocently*): Where's who?

NIGHTSHADE: I don't have time for games. The Prince, that's who.

BARBARA: Uh . . . I think he went to a movie. A double feature. He probably won't be back for a couple of hours. Would you like to come back later?

JACK: I'm afraid it's no good, Barbara. She knows he's here.

BARBARA: But, Jack—

JACK: She's got us this time.

NIGHTSHADE: He's right. (*To* BARBARA) Where's the Prince?

BARBARA: He's in the kitchen.

NIGHTSHADE: Get him. (BARBARA *gives* JACK *questioning look.*)

JACK: Better do as she says, Barbara.

BARBARA (*Crossing right; calling off*): Excuse me, sir? There's—um—someone here to see you. (*After a moment,* PRINCE, *apron tied around his waist, enters.*)

NIGHTSHADE: So? Where is he?

BARBARA: What do you mean, where is he? He's right there.

NIGHTSHADE: I mean the Prince.

BARBARA: But this *is* the Prince. (*She looks at* "PRINCE," *who is shaking his head*.) You mean you're not the Prince?

JACK (*Pointing*): This is Otis, the Prince's trusted secretary and valet. The real Prince Babbaloney is—

OTIS/PRINCE (*Entering upstage*): Right here.

BARBARA: Oh, my gosh. I don't believe this.

NIGHTSHADE: Good. You saved me the trouble of coming to look for you. (*During next exchange, real* PRINCE *strolls left. In order to keep her gun on him,* NIGHTSHADE *is forced to keep turning, so that eventually her back is to* BARBARA.)

PRINCE: And now that you have me, what are you going to do?

NIGHTSHADE: Why, stop you from testifying tomorrow, of course.

PRINCE: But they already have the evidence they need. My appearance before the committee is only a formality.

NIGHTSHADE: You're bluffing.

PRINCE: Are you sure?

NIGHTSHADE: Of course I'm sure. Why else would the agency go to this much trouble to hide you?

PRINCE: How do you know this is not a trap?

NIGHTSHADE: A trap? Ha! I'm too smart to be trapped by the likes of you! (BARBARA *suddenly leans forward, grabs pillow off chair and bops* NIGHTSHADE *on the head.* NIGHTSHADE, *thrown off balance, falls to floor*.)

JACK: Nice work! (*Takes handcuffs from pocket, puts them on* NIGHTSHADE *as she struggles up*)

BARBARA: Are you O.K., Your Highness?

PRINCE: Thanks to you, Miss Turner. (*Crosses to her and kisses her hand*) I owe you my life. (JACK *looks on, jealous*.)

JACK (*Quickly*): And I owe you dinner. How about tomorrow night?

BARBARA (*Flustered; looking from* PRINCE *to* JACK): Well . . . (*Phone ringing is heard.* JACK *pulls banana from his pocket.*)

JACK (*To* BARBARA): Wait! Hold that thought. (*Speaking into banana*) Yes, Chief? . . . No, everything's fine. And good news—we've finally caught Nightshade. (*Continues to pantomime phone conversation*)

MOTHER (*Entering right; to* OTIS): Oh, there you are, young man. (*She takes his arm to lead him right. Just before they exit, she looks back at others, realizing there's something very strange about the scene—the handcuffed* NIGHTSHADE, PRINCE *still holding* BARBARA's *hand, and* JACK *holding banana to his ear.* MOTHER *shrugs, and* BARBARA *smiles awkwardly.*)

MYRNA (*Entering through open door left, nonplussed by what she sees*): Hi, Barbara. Ready to go? (JACK *finishes conversation, puts banana back in pocket.*)

BARBARA: Thanks anyway, Myrna, but I think I'll just spend a quiet evening at home . . . with friends.

MYRNA (*Sighing*): Suit yourself. (*Turns to go*) You'll never know what you're missing. (*Exits.* BARBARA *and* JACK *look at each other and laugh as curtain closes.*)

THE END

PRODUCTION NOTES

SECRET AGENTS IN DISGUISE

Characters: 3 male; 4 female (Claire/Nightshade can be played by same person)

Playing Time: 30 minutes.

Costumes: Trench coats, white fedoras, dark glasses for Jack and Claire; Myrna's hair is purple. She wears black shirt and miniskirt, boots, chain belt, and lots of unusual jewelry. Barbara wears skirt, sweater, and heels. Mother wears dress. "Otis" wears suit and glasses; "Prince" wears bright African wrap and gold chains; Nightshade wears black fedora and trench coat.

Setting: Scene 1, produce section of grocery store. At center is counter with fresh fruit. Upstage and on either side are display racks of various grocery items. Scene 2, living room. Sofa is center, coffee table with phone, armchairs. At left is working front door. Exit upstage to rest of house; exit right to kitchen.

Properties: Banana; shopping cart; shopping list; wallet; two bags of groceries; mixing bowl and spoon; bag containing Chinese food; handcuffs.

Sound: Ringing phone; doorbell; explosion.

Lighting: Lights may flash during explosion.

Where There's a Will, There's a Play

Characters

WILL SHAKESPEARE, *struggling writer*
ANNE, his wife
OPHELIA JONES
FRANK MACBETH
DESDEMONA MOORE } *their neighbors*
ROMEO MONTAGUE
JULIET CAPULET

TIME: *Morning in spring, late 1500s.*
SETTING: *Main room of the Shakespeares' modest cottage in the London suburbs, furnished with plain furniture typical of the 16th century. A large desk center dominates the stage; on it are large reference books, quill and ink pot, and paper, much of it crumpled into messy balls. At left is hallway to cooking area. Up right is dutch door leading outside.*
AT RISE: WILL SHAKESPEARE *is seated at desk, writing very quickly.* ANNE *enters left, carrying tray of bread and fruit, and a mug. She crosses to desk and sets tray down.*

ANNE: How is the writing coming today, my love? (WILL *groans, crumples paper;* ANNE *sighs.*) Never mind.

WILL: The most dire of human afflictions has cursed me.

ANNE: Pray tell.

WILL: Writer's block. Nary a clever tale or wicked plot has graced these pages in a fortnight. (*Takes her hand*) What am I to do, Anne?

ANNE (*Handing him mug*): First, you must have some refreshment. Perhaps on the morrow the stories will start to come once more. (*She crosses to door.*)

WILL: And if not? Would you think me a failure?

ANNE (*Smiling*): The course of true love never did run smooth. (*She opens the top half of door.*) Perhaps the breeze of morning will inspire you. (*As she starts to walk left,* OPHELIA *appears at door.*)

OPHELIA: Anne!

ANNE (*Turning, crossing to door*): Ophelia! What a lovely surprise! (*Opens door to let* OPHELIA *in.*)

OPHELIA (*Distraught*): Have you a moment, dear friend? My heart is in need of advice. (*While the two women talk,* WILL *writes, crumples and discards pages.*)

ANNE: Speak the speech, I pray you. Is something wrong?

OPHELIA: It is the man I've spoken of, the one who holds my heart.

ANNE: Hamlet, is it not? The young man from Denmark?

OPHELIA (*Nodding*): A prince of a fellow.

ANNE: Then what troubles you?

OPHELIA (*Hesitantly*): He has a most peculiar habit, Anne. Most recently, I've overheard him talking to a skull!

ANNE: What!

OPHELIA: Worse yet, when I confronted him, he denied it, telling me, "It is my father to whom I speak."

ANNE (*Puzzled*): But his father is dead, is he not?

OPHELIA: Yes, but according to Hamlet, his father's spirit

still lingers on the battlements. I tried to suggest, ever so gently, that dear Hamlet seek help.

ANNE: And what did he say?

OPHELIA (*Crying*): He told me to get myself to a nunnery! (*As* ANNE *consoles* OPHELIA, WILL *looks up in exasperation, clears his throat.*)

ANNE (*Nervously*): Perhaps we should continue this in the next room, Ophelia. William needs to concentrate on the manuscript his publisher is awaiting.

OPHELIA: A thousand pardons, William. I did not mean to disturb you. (OPHELIA *and* ANNE *exit left.* FRANK MACBETH *rushes in right.*)

FRANK: Will! Thank heavens you're here!

WILL (*Barely looking up*): Greetings, Frank, though your arrival is ill-timed.

FRANK (*Pulling up chair, sitting at desk*): I'll be only a minute.

WILL: Very well. What is on your mind?

FRANK: Lady Macbeth and I are entertaining my boss this evening. You remember Duncan, do you not?

WILL: Of course. What of him?

FRANK: A dreadful plot's afoot, I fear, and my scheming wife is behind it.

WILL (*With interest*): What is it that has you so distraught?

FRANK: Lady Macbeth seeks to get me Duncan's title by means most foul. (*Shakes his head*) I dread this coming night and its consequences. What am I to do, Will?

WILL: Surely you exaggerate. All's well that ends well. You'll see. Perhaps a walk in Dunsinane Woods will clear your head.

FRANK (*Inspired*): Yes, of course! And I could take Spot with me. Your words have reassured me. (*As* FRANK *exits right,* ANNE *and* OPHELIA *reenter left.*)

ANNE: There are other fish in the sea, Ophelia.

OPHELIA: But how shall I forget him, Anne?

ANNE: By staying busy, having a good time. The beauty of the day awaits. (*Looks out door*) Today is a lovely day, in fact, for a swim.

OPHELIA: What a grand idea! Thank you! (*She starts to exit right, nearly colliding with* DESDEMONA.) Desdemona! I'd love to stay and chat, but I must be off. (*She exits.*)

DESDEMONA (*Calling after* OPHELIA): Greetings, Ophelia! (*Turns to* ANNE) Have you a moment, Anne?

ANNE: Most certainly. Have you time for tea?

DESDEMONA: My absence, I fear, would test my husband's patience. He's grown quite suspicious of late.

ANNE: Yet he adores you above all others.

DESDEMONA (*Confidentially*): It's Iago, I'd wager, who's behind our troubles.

ANNE: Iago? That little twit? What, pray tell, has he done now?

DESDEMONA: He fuels the fires of jealousy, Anne. I dread to think each day what he may do to destroy my marriage. Only yesterday, Othello looked at me as if he wanted to strangle me.

ANNE: Oh, dear!

DESDEMONA: But enough sad talk. I've come to borrow a scarf.

ANNE: You want to borrow a scarf from me? But your closets are brimming with clothes that Othello has brought you from distant shores.

DESDEMONA: True. But I have lost one that is most special, Anne. I should die if he learned I had misplaced it. You have one that is similar, I believe.

ANNE: Then let us look, if it will help. (*They exit left.* ROMEO *and* JULIET *enter right.*)

ROMEO (*Gesturing to* WILL): Thank goodness, he's here!

JULIET: Perhaps he can aid us.

ROMEO: Excuse me, Mr. Shakespeare.

WILL (*Looking up*): Oh, hello, Romeo. (*Rises from desk*) And who is this?

ROMEO: Juliet of Capulet. (JULIET *curtsies*.)

WILL (*Bowing*): I'm charmed.

ROMEO: We are in dire need of your advice. Although we met only last week, Juliet and I wish to marry.

WILL: Such haste would be foolish, would it not?

JULIET: But we're in love, sir.

ROMEO: We've come to ask you a question of great importance.

WILL: Why ask me? It is the houses of Montague and Capulet whose blessing you must seek, not mine.

ROMEO: Ay, there's the rub, sir.

JULIET: Our families are mortal enemies. We shall never receive their blessing.

WILL: And how do you think I can help you?

ROMEO (*Humbly*): We shall need a purse of gold, sir, to help us elope.

WILL (*Sighing*): What fools these mortals be!

ROMEO: Surely there is no harm in borrowing, sir?

WILL: Neither a borrower nor a lender be, Romeo, for a fool and his money are soon parted.

ROMEO (*To* JULIET): Alas, we must ask someone else to help us in our plight. (*They exit.* WILL *shakes his head, turns back to his writing.* ANNE *and* DESDEMONA *enter left;* DESDEMONA *is tying bright scarf around her neck, and* ANNE *carries two letters.*)

ANNE: But Desdemona, this scarf isn't the same color as the one you've lost, is it?

DESDEMONA: No. I'm hoping Othello won't notice. (*As she exits right*) Let's have lunch next week, Anne.

WILL (*Looking up*): Lunch? That reminds me, Anne. Is it not today that Lear is joining us for lunch?

ANNE (*Handing him letters*): His letter this date states otherwise. (WILL *opens letter and begins to read.*)

WILL (*After he has finished reading*): How strange that he has decided to take his midday meal with an attorney instead of with us!

ANNE: Not so strange at that, Will. He frets about the state of his kingdom and how to divide it among his three daughters.

WILL: Ah, yes! Those greedy girls. He'd do well to leave them nothing at all.

ANNE: Who wrote the other letter?

WILL (*Looking at envelope*): Great Caesar's Ghost! I recognize that hand.

ANNE: It looks like Greek to me.

WILL (*Opening letter*): Not Greek, but Roman. (*Reads*) Well, well, it seems as if Julius Caesar seeks my assistance for a speech he must give.

ANNE: How splendid! When?

WILL: The Ides of March. A gathering, it appears, of friends, Romans, and countrymen.

ANNE: But what of your plays, Will? When will you find the time to write them?

WILL: To be honest, Anne, I believe I have found an answer. (*Rises from desk and takes her hand*) Have you the name of the real estate agent who showed us the cottage at Stratford-on-Avon last month?

ANNE: Most certainly I have it, but why do you ask?

WILL: Our neighbors here prove endless distraction from my work. The time has come, my love, for us to leave London. The cottage we saw would be perfect for my verses and your roses.

ANNE (*Embracing* WILL): Oh, Will, how sweet! I know we would be most happy there!

WILL: Come, let's don our finery and visit our new dwelling.

ANNE (*As they cross slowly left*): A fine idea, Will!

WILL: And perhaps we can attend a show, as well. I told you, did I not, of the new theater in town? The Globe, I believe it is called.

ANNE: Why, just think, Will. Perhaps someday your plays will be performed there.

WILL: A pleasant thought, dear wife. I'll make inquiry at the Globe while we're there. (*They exit, talking excitedly. Quick curtain*)

THE END

PRODUCTION NOTES

WHERE THERE'S A WILL, THERE'S A PLAY

Characters: 3 male; 4 female.

Playing Time: 15 minutes.

Costumes: Elizabethan dress.

Setting: Main room of the Shakespeares' modest cottage in the London suburbs, furnished with plain furniture typical of the 16th century. A large desk center dominates stage; on it are large reference books, quill and ink pot, and paper, much of it crumpled into messy balls. At left is hallway to rest of house. Up right is dutch door leading outside.

Properties: Tray of food, mug, brightly colored scarf, two letters.

Lighting and Sound: No special effects.

Eat, Drink, and Be Scary

Characters

MAVIS ⎫ *owners of "Bumps" restaurant*
HILDY ⎭
ELISE, *Mavis' daughter*
EVAN STEELBURG, *Elise's guest*
FRANK, *clumsy busboy*
MAX, *dishwasher*
DRAKE, *maitre d'*
MARGARET
PHYLLIS
FRIEDA ⎬ *patrons*
T. J. McCARDLE
RUMPELSTILTSKIN
ANNIE

TIME: *The present.*
SETTING: *"Bumps" restaurant, decorated with hanging bats and spider webs. Four dining tables covered with black tablecloths (reverse side of tablecloths is white) and jack-o-lanterns are left. Podium draped in black cloth with skull pencil holder is right. Exit at right of podium leads outside. Exit to banquet room is left; skeleton hangs on wall beside entrance. Sign above stage reads,* WELCOME TO BUMPS IN THE NIGHT. WE SERVE SPIRITS.

AT RISE: MAVIS, *dressed in witch garb, rushes about, throwing jack-o-lanterns in box and reversing tablecloths to white side. With alarm, she spots spider webs on ceiling, pulls handkerchief from pocket, and stands on chair to brush webs away. HILDY, also in witch dress, enters right, studying list.*

HILDY (*Alarmed*): Mavis! What are you doing? Our spiders spent all day spinning those!

MAVIS: Well, they've all got to come down in the next ten minutes, or I'm ruined!

HILDY: Ruined? Good grief, Mavis, what's come over you?

MAVIS (*Stepping down from chair to resume tidying*): Motherhood, that's what. My daughter, Elise, just called.

HILDY: From UCLA? That's nice.

MAVIS: From across town. That's terrible.

HILDY (*Putting list on podium*): Terrible? But you adore her. (*Puzzled*) And what's she doing in town?

MAVIS: She just flew in . . . by plane. (*Walks to skeleton on wall*)

HILDY (*In disparaging tone*): Plane, hmm? No self-respecting witch would get into one of those. (*Shakes head*) There are easier ways to fly!

MAVIS: Give me a hand with Merrill, will you, Hildy? (*Takes down skeleton*) This old bag of bones weighs more than he looks.

HILDY (*Taking skeleton, cradling it*): What am I supposed to do with him?

MAVIS: Put him in the closet. No one will ever look there. (*Harried*) They'll be here any minute, and this place still doesn't look normal. (*She crosses stage and hides pencil holder under podium and pulls off the cloth.*)

HILDY: Normal? Why should it? (*Sets skeleton in chair and crosses to* MAVIS) Mavis, will you please tell me what's going on?

MAVIS: Elise is bringing someone here for dinner tonight.

HILDY (*Shrugging*): The more, the scarier, that's what I always say. So, does this someone have a name?

MAVIS: Evan Something-or-Other. Elise met him in one of her film classes and she hasn't stopped talking about him. (*She takes vases of flowers from box, starts putting them on tables.*)

HILDY: Hmm . . . is it serious?

MAVIS: I think so. Elise says they want to ask me something very important.

HILDY (*Delighted*): Sounds like wedding bells to me!

MAVIS: Not if he sees this place. That's why we have to make it look normal by six o'clock.

HILDY (*Cautiously*): You mean he's not . . . one of us?

MAVIS: Well, Hildy, neither is Elise, really. I mean, not a hundred percent. (*Shrugs*) The drawback of marrying a mortal, I guess. She always took after her father.

HILDY: Why can't they meet you someplace else?

MAVIS: Elise says it has to be here. As soon as he takes one look at the help . . . (*At that moment, FRANK and MAX enter right. FRANK is a dead ringer for Frankenstein's monster; on a leash, following close behind, is MAX, a werewolf. They cross stage and exit up left.*)

HILDY: Maybe Evan won't notice.

MAVIS: How could you not notice a green busboy who drops things and a dishwasher who howls at the moon? (*Snaps fingers*) I know! Let's give Frank and Max the night off!

HILDY: No way! We'd run ourselves ragged.

MAVIS: So maybe it will be slow.

HILDY: On Saturday? Mavis, we're completely booked!

MAVIS: Rats! Well, maybe we can have Drake seat everybody back in the banquet room and put Elise and her young man out here by themselves.

HILDY (*Looking at her watch*): Where is Drake, anyway? He

should have been up twenty minutes ago. (*On cue*, DRAKE *enters. He is dressed stylishly in tuxedo and red-satin-lined cape. He also has red lips and slicked-back hair.*)

DRAKE: Did I hear my name?

HILDY (*Sarcastically*): Did you hear your alarm? It's almost six.

DRAKE: Blame it on the sunset. (*Crosses to podium, stands behind it*)

MAVIS (*Urgently*): Drake, I need a favor.

DRAKE: So do I. How about some fresh dirt in my coffin? (*Squirms*) That last batch had gravel in it.

MAVIS: O.K., O.K. Listen, I want you to seat all of the regulars in the back room tonight.

DRAKE (*Eyebrows raised*): They're not going to like that.

MAVIS: It's just for tonight. (*Sound of eerie organ music is heard.*) Oh, dear! Do you think the Phantom could play something a bit more cheery?

HILDY (*Shrugging*): I can always ask. (*Exits up left*)

DRAKE (*Looking around podium, not finding what he wants*): Hildy forgot to tell me what the special is tonight.

MAVIS: Steak and garlic. (DRAKE *gasps*; MAVIS *smiles.*) Just kidding. Oh, I'd better tell Frank and Max to keep a low profile tonight. (*She exits; music screeches to a stop, then goes into medley of slow, soft rock songs.* MARGARET *and* PHYLLIS *enter in witch attire and pointed hats; they are in the middle of conversation.*)

MARGARET: So then that icky Snow White took one bite of it and was flat on her back before you could say, "Boo!"

PHYLLIS: Really? Why, that's almost as good as when I put a whole kingdom to sleep!

DRAKE: Table for two, ladies?

PHYLLIS: Three, actually. (*Checks watch*) Frieda's joining us, but she's always late.

MARGARET (*Pointing*): The table over there will be fine.

DRAKE: I'm sorry. It's taken.

PHYLLIS: How about the one next to it?

DRAKE: I'm afraid they're all reserved this evening, ladies. But I do have a dark booth in the back.

MARGARET (*Disappointed*): Well, if that's the best you can do. (FRIEDA, *quite disheveled, rushes on.*) Oh, Frieda! We were worried about you.

PHYLLIS: Where were you?

FRIEDA: My broom stalled out over Cleveland.

MARGARET: Cleveland? Isn't that a tad out of your way?

FRIEDA: Well, I had some nasty business to clear up out there.

PHYLLIS: What was that?

DRAKE (*Picking up menus and leading the way up left*): Would you follow me, ladies? (*Starts to exit left*)

FRIEDA: Well, you remember those gingerbread cookies I sent everyone last Christmas?

MARGARET: The ones that looked like little people?

PHYLLIS *and* MARGARET (*Ad lib as they exit*): My, they were delicious! Yes, indeed! (*Etc. All exit.* RUMPELSTIL-TSKIN, *in troll's costume, and* ANNIE, *another witch, enter and stand by podium.*)

RUMPELSTILTSKIN: So I said, "Sure, no problem." I'll have all this straw spun into gold by, say, ten tomorrow morning.

ANNIE: But you said she was poor. How was she going to pay you?

RUMPELSTILTSKIN: That's the beauty of it. She promised to give me her first-born child when she married the king.

ANNIE (*Shaking head*): Big mistake, kiddo. Take it from me. Ask for anything, but not the first-born child!

RUMPELSTILTSKIN: No kidding. Problems?

ANNIE: Night and day. I mean, I made the same kind of bargain: I thought I could keep the kid up in this big tower so she wouldn't get into any trouble. Well, no such luck.

RUMPELSTILTSKIN: What happened? (DRAKE *reenters.*)

ANNIE: Well, she grew this incredibly long hair. I mean, so long she can throw it out the window, and it goes all the way to the ground.

RUMPELSTILTSKIN: You're kidding.

ANNIE: At first it was convenient, since I don't have an elevator.

RUMPELSTILTSKIN: Sounds practical to me.

ANNIE: It was, until she started using all that goop on it. If I'm not knee-deep in mousse, I get stuck halfway down in hairspray. Last night, though, was the worst. She used a new conditioner that made her hair so silky and slippery, I nearly lost my grip and fell through the sidewalk!

DRAKE: Table for two, sir?

RUMPELSTILTSKIN: Yes, please.

DRAKE: This way, please. (*Starts to exit left*)

RUMPELSTILTSKIN (*As they walk by skeleton on chair*): What happened to him?

DRAKE (*Matter-of-factly*): People are dying to get in here. (*Exits; ANNIE and RUMPELSTILTSKIN follow. After a moment, MAVIS enters up left as T. J. McCARDLE enters right. T. J. wears suit, hat, and carries briefcase.*)

MAVIS (*Surprised*): T.J.! Is that really you?

T.J.: Straight off the Concorde. How do I look?

MAVIS (*Diplomatically*): Well, it's not my style, but I understand that look is quite fashionable in some groups.

T.J.: Mavis, image is everything. (*Withdraws business card, passes it to MAVIS*)

MAVIS (*Reading*): T.J. McCardle, M.B.A.

T.J. (*Interpreting*): Magic by Appointment. No more fly-by-night jobs for me.

MAVIS: Well, you certainly look successful.

T.J.: And worthy of your best seat in the house. (DRAKE *reenters. T.J. points to empty table.*) How about that one over there?

MAVIS (*Quickly*): I'm afraid it's taken, T.J.

T.J.: By whom? The invisible man?

MAVIS (*Apologizing*): We're really busy tonight, T.J. (HILDY *reenters*.) You wouldn't mind sitting in the back, would you?

T.J. (*Laughing*): Oh, really, Mavis! People come here to Bumps to be seen! Besides (*Indicates briefcase*), I've got to prepare for a meeting at midnight, and it's too dark in the back to work. (*Sails past* DRAKE *to table*) No need for a menu, Drake. I'll have the Black Magic Snails on rice and the hemlock salad. (*Sits, opens briefcase, and starts working*)

DRAKE: Would you like anything to drink, madam?

T.J.: What goes with snails?

DRAKE: May I recommend something red, properly served at 98.6 degrees? (*With a sly smile*) I speak from experience.

T.J.: You're a man after my own heart. (*Returns to work;* DRAKE *exits.*)

MAVIS (*To* HILDY): Oh, dear! And it was going so well.

HILDY: Will you relax? I'm sure she'll just keep to herself.

MAVIS (*Sighing*): I guess so. How's it going in the kitchen? (*Loud crash of breaking dishes offstage*)

HILDY: Same as always. (*Loud wolf howls offstage*)

MAVIS: Oh, no! I forgot it was a full moon. Can't we put a muzzle on Max until Elise and her boyfriend leave?

HILDY: Let's tell him it's the neighbor's dog (MAX *enters, howling, as he dries dishes.*), and that he knows a lot of tricks. (*Sound of horn honking;* MAVIS *runs to look off right.*)

MAVIS: They're here!

HILDY (*Taking* MAX *and leading him off left*): Come on, Max. I'll give you some table scraps. (MAVIS *watches anxiously as they exit.* ELISE *enters. She wears skirt and sweater.*)

ELISE: Mama! (*Runs to give her a hug*)

MAVIS: Elise, dear! It's so good to see you! (*During this exchange,* DRAKE *enters, carrying wine glass of tomato juice, which he serves to* T.J. MAVIS *looks about anxiously.*) So where's Evan?

ELISE: He's parking the car. I can hardly wait for you two to meet.

MAVIS: Wonderful. Why don't we all meet for lunch tomorrow?

ELISE: Tomorrow? Oh, Mama, don't be silly. We came all this way to have dinner with you tonight.

MAVIS: Yes, dear, but, uh . . . tonight's really busy.

ELISE (*Looking around; puzzled*): Busy?

MAVIS: It's going to be. You know how these full moons can be. I'll be lucky to catch my breath for two minutes.

ELISE: But, Mama, two minutes is all we need.

MAVIS (*Squeezing her hand*): Whatever it is, Elise, it's fine with me. The important thing is that Evan asked you. He did ask you, didn't he?

ELISE (*Nodding*): Yesterday afternoon.

MAVIS: And you said . . . ?

ELISE: I said only if my mother agreed to it.

MAVIS (*Earnestly*): Elise, dear, would this make you happy?

ELISE: Out of this world, Mama.

MAVIS (*Embracing* ELISE): Wonderful! Well, now that we're both happy, I'd better get back to work. (FRANK *enters with stack of dishes.*)

ELISE (*Waving to* FRANK): Frank! (*Pleased to see her,* FRANK *drops dishes and walks stiffly over to give her a hug*) How are you doing, Tall, Green, and Handsome? (FRANK *beams. Barking is heard offstage;* MAX *and* HILDY, *engaged in tug-of-war with dish towel, back onto stage.* MAX *yanks towel away and runs out right.*)

HILDY: Max! Max! You come back here right . . . (*Stops in*

her tracks) Oh, hello, Elise. (EVAN *is entering just as*
MAX *runs past him.* HILDY *smiles at him, then exits
after* MAX.)

EVAN (*Looking around in amazement*): So this is it?

MAVIS (*Exasperated*): This is it, all right. (FRANK *starts
to pick up dishes.*)

ELISE: Evan, come and meet Mama. Mama, I want you to
meet Evan Steelburg.

EVAN: Pleased to meet you, Mrs. Bumps. I suppose Elise
told you why I'm here.

ELISE (*To* EVAN): I thought you'd like to ask her yourself.
She has the final say, you know.

EVAN: Sure. Well . . . (*Before he can continue,* MARGA-
RET, PHYLLIS, *and* FRIEDA, *carrying plates of food,
enter left and approach one of the tables.*)

MARGARET: See? There's plenty of room out here. Let's
take this table. (FRANK *exits with dishes.*)

PHYLLIS: Good idea. Now, where was I?

FRIEDA (*As they sit*): You had just turned him into a frog.

PHYLLIS: Warts and all! (*They all laugh.*)

T.J.: Would you mind keeping it down over there? I'm trying
to do some work.

FRIEDA (*Looking over in astonishment*): T.J. McCardle? Is
that you?

T.J.: Frieda? Frieda Lippincott! (FRIEDA *runs over, embraces* T.J.) My goodness, it's been centuries, hasn't it?

FRIEDA (*To* MARGARET *and* PHYLLIS): Back in a minute, girls. (*Sits with* T.J.) So, what have you been up to?
(*They pantomime conversation.*)

ANNIE (*As she and* RUMPELSTILTSKIN *enter with
plates*): As I said, kids today are nothing but problems. If
I had it to do over, I'd hold out for the first million or the
first villa in Spain. But the firstborn child, never!

RUMPELSTILTSKIN (*Indicating table where skeleton sits*):

How about this one? (*To skeleton*) Mind if we join you? (RUMPELSTILTSKIN *and* ANNIE *sit and talk in pantomime.* HILDY *enters, catches* MAVIS's *eye, shrugs.*)

MAVIS (*Nervously; turning quickly to* EVAN): Believe me, I can explain everything.

EVAN: No need, Mrs. Bumps. All I want to hear is your answer. Is it yes?

MAVIS: You mean, in spite of everything, you still want . . .

EVAN: Oh, there are still a few obstacles. I knew there would be. But it's nothing we can't work out.

MAVIS (*Surprised*): You're serious?

EVAN: Of course I'm serious. This is the chance of a lifetime. As soon as Elise told me about you, I knew this would be perfect.

MAVIS: Well, if Elise is happy, I'm happy.

EVAN: Now, we have a lot of details to work out. I don't want this to interfere with your work.

MAVIS: Elise's happiness is my first priority. What can I do to help?

EVAN (*Looking around*): Well, we'd like to do the whole thing here.

HILDY: Oh, Mavis! How exciting! Can I make the cake?

EVAN: Cake sounds terrific, but I really don't want any of you to go to a lot of extra trouble.

MAVIS: No trouble at all. Whatever you and Elise want.

EVAN (*Checking out the room*): We'll have to move some of the furniture, of course. But don't worry . . . we'll put it all back.

MAVIS: No problem.

EVAN (*Noticing other diners*): Now, about those people. . . .

MAVIS: Oh, they'll be gone, I promise.

EVAN: No, no! They're perfect. Do you think they'd like to be involved, too?

MAVIS (*Hesitating*): Well . . .

HILDY: You have to admit we do treat our customers as if they're family, Mavis.

MAVIS: I suppose I could ask.

EVAN: I'll be happy to pay them, if that's the problem.

MAVIS: Oh, my goodness! That's very generous, Evan, I must say, but payment is out of the question.

EVAN: Whatever you say, Mrs. Bumps.

ELISE (*To* EVAN): We haven't told her the dates.

EVAN: Oh, you're right. (*To* MAVIS) Well, if it's O.K. with you, we'd like to get this show on the road on the 24th.

MAVIS (*Surprised*): That's awfully short notice.

EVAN: Time is money, Mrs. Bumps. If everything goes well, I'd like to see this thing end by the 10th.

HILDY (*Confused*): I beg your pardon?

MAVIS: See what end?

EVAN (*Shrugging*): What we've been talking about. Two weeks is about right. Three is really stretching it, don't you think?

MAVIS (*Upset*): I thought you were talking about a lifetime.

EVAN: Well, they used to take that long in the old days. Modern technology, though, and it can be over like (*Snaps fingers*) that.

MAVIS (*To* ELISE): Elise, I think you and I should have a talk.

ELISE (*In reassuring tone*): Mama, the sooner we start it, the sooner we can end it.

MAVIS: And why are you in such a hurry to end it?

EVAN: Because I've already got my next one lined up.

MAVIS (*Horrified; shouting her next line, which is accompanied by crash of thunder and flickering lights*): What?! (*All on stage suddenly fall silent.*)

ELISE (*Upset*): Mama, take it easy.

EVAN (*Impressed*): Wow! Did you just do that with the lights and thunder?

MAVIS (*Imperiously*): That, young man, is just the beginning. (*Hands on hips*) I withdraw my consent.

ELISE (*Protesting*): Mama!

MAVIS (*To* ELISE): We may not be the most perfect family, Elise, but if there's one thing I've always taught you, it's that you deserve a happy-ever-after. Now, they're not always easy to come by, but the search is worth it. I've never told you what to do, dear, but in this case, it's for your own good. I absolutely, positively, unequivocally forbid you to get married. (*All except* ELISE *and* EVAN *applaud.*)

ELISE (*Stunned*): Mama, I'm not getting married!

MAVIS (*Pleased*): Good girl. I'm glad you changed your mind.

ELISE: Changed my mind? But it wasn't made up.

MAVIS: But you said you told him yes.

ELISE (*Explaining*): Mama, I told him yes, I thought it would be O.K. if he made a movie in the restaurant.

ALL (*Surprised*): A movie!

MAVIS (*Pointing to* EVAN): Him?

ELISE (*Annoyed*): Of course, him! It's not every day you get an offer like that from Evan Steelburg!

ALL (*Together*): Evan Steelburg! (*All rush over to* EVAN *to ask for autographs, auditions, etc.*)

MAVIS (*Crossing downstage with* ELISE; *in questioning tone*): Evan Steelburg?

ELISE: Mama, he's a famous movie producer! You know, "Back to the Suture"? "The Color Chartreuse"? "E.P."?

MAVIS (*Thinking for a moment, then shrugging*): I knew that. (*She and* ELISE *laugh and hug as curtain closes.*)

THE END

PRODUCTION NOTES

EAT, DRINK, AND BE SCARY

Characters: 8 female; 5 male.

Playing Time: 20 minutes.

Costumes: Traditional black witch dresses and hats for Mavis, Hildy, Margaret, Phyllis, Frieda, and Annie. Suit and stylish hat for T.J. Frankenstein costume for Frank. Werewolf fur for Max. Dracula costume for Drake. "Troll" attire for Rumpelstiltskin. Everyday dress for Elise and Evan.

Properties: Reservation list; leash; briefcase; business card; stack of dishes; dish towel; plates of food.

Setting: Bumps Restaurant, decorated with hanging bats and spider webs. Four dining tables covered with black tablecloths (reverse side of tablecloths is white) and jack-o-lanterns are left. Podium draped in black cloth with skull pencil holder is right. Exit at right of podium leads outside. Exit to banquet room is left; skeleton hangs on wall beside entrance. Sign above stage reads, WELCOME TO BUMPS IN THE NIGHT. WE SERVE SPIRITS.

Lighting: Flash of lightning.

Sound: Eerie organ music; soft rock music; barking; horn honking; crash of thunder.

Mother Goose Gumshoe

Characters

SCOOP SNOOPINS, *finder of lost characters*
ZELLA COURT, *his trusted secretary*
MRS. DUMPTY ⎱
MRS. COBBLER ⎬ *clients*
MRS. PIPER ⎰

TIME: *The present.*
SETTING: *Scoop Snoopins' office. His desk is center—it has a phone, bulging file folders, telephone books, maps of the city, etc. Chairs for clients are up right of desk. File cabinets are left. Two trench coats and a hat are on coat tree, up right, and exit is right.*
AT RISE: SCOOP SNOOPINS *is busy at his desk when phone rings. He answers.*
SCOOP (*Into phone*): Scoop Snoopins Lost and Found Detective Agency. May I help you? (*Reaches for paper and pencil*) Uh-huh. . . . Uh-huh. . . . O. K., Mr. Hubbard, let's take this from the top. (*Writes*) You say your wife went to the cupboard this morning? . . . And why did she do that? . . . To get your dog a bone, I see. Then what happened, Mr. Hubbard? . . . The cupboard was bare, hmm? . . .And that's when she disappeared? Well, this may be just a shot in the dark, but is it possible that she went

to the grocery store? I may be totally wrong, of course, but from what you've told me, the evidence seems to be pointing in that direction. The missing station wagon, the missing checkbook, the cents-off coupons missing from the food section of the paper all seem to indicate that shopping was on her mind. (ZELLA *enters and hangs up coat.*) Well, listen, Mr. Hubbard, if she's not back in an hour, call me and we'll take it from there. No problem—any time. (*Hangs up, looks at* ZELLA) Morning, Zella.

ZELLA: Morning, Scoop. You're here early.

SCOOP: Looks as if it's going to be a busy day. (*Hands her folders*) Do you mind wrapping up the paperwork on the Curds and Whey Affair?

ZELLA (*Pleased*): So you found out why the Muffet Girl ran away?

SCOOP (*Nodding*): Thanks to the anonymous tip about those spiders on Tuffets Landing. Seems that one set down beside Miss Muffet and scared her out of her wits. She's O.K. now. (MRS. DUMPTY, *carrying purse, rushes in.*)

MRS. DUMPTY: Oh, thank goodness you're here!

SCOOP: Can we help you?

MRS. DUMPTY: I'm missing someone.

ZELLA: Then you've come to the right place.

SCOOP: Who is missing, ma'am?

MRS. DUMPTY: My husband. One minute, he was just sitting on the garden wall and in the very next, he was gone!

SCOOP (*Gesturing toward chair*): Why don't you have a seat, Mrs. . . .

MRS. DUMPTY: Dumpty. Mrs. H. Dumpty. (*Sits*)

SCOOP (*Taking notes*): What's your husband's name, Mrs. Dumpty?

MRS. DUMPTY: Humpty. Middle initial "A," for Arnold.

ZELLA: Do you have a picture of him?

MRS. DUMPTY: Right here in my purse. (*Takes photo from purse, hands it to* ZELLA) I took it last Easter.

SCOOP: Hm-m-m. He looks like a good egg to me . . . not the sort to run off.

MRS. DUMPTY: I'm so upset—I don't know what to do!

SCOOP: Just start with the facts, ma'am.

MRS. DUMPTY: Well, it was a hot day, so hot you could fry eggs on the sidewalk. Humpty was sitting outside, talking to the neighbors, and—(*Sobs*)

ZELLA (*Patting her shoulder*): There, there, don't go to pieces. If anyone can find your husband, it's Scoop Snoopins.

SCOOP: She's right, Mrs. Dumpty—I've unscrambled some of the toughest. Now, this may be a hard case to crack, but don't worry about a thing.

MRS. DUMPTY: But what if something terrible happened? What if he took a bad fall?

SCOOP: Well, he may be shell-shocked for a while, but—

ZELLA: Excuse me, Mrs. Dumpty, but did you check the other side of the wall?

MRS. DUMPTY (*Sobbing*): No.

ZELLA: Isn't it possible he could have simply rolled off?

MRS. DUMPTY: An egg roll? Yes, I suppose it's entirely possible.

SCOOP: Well, then, I suggest you put in a call immediately to all the king's horses and all the king's men. (*Aside; grimly*) You may need them. Meantime, keep your sunny side up!

MRS. DUMPTY (*Shaking his hand*): Thank you, Mr. Snoopins. I appreciate your help. (*Exits*)

MRS. COBBLER (*Entering*): Is this the Scoop Snoopins Agency?

SCOOP: Sure is. How can we help you? (*Gestures to chair*) Please, have a seat.

MRS. COBBLER (*Crossing to sit down*): It's my children.

ZELLA: Are they lost?

MRS. COBBLER: I'm not sure. (*Upset*) You see, I have so many of them, I don't know what to do.

SCOOP: Let's start from the beginning. First of all, what's your name?

MRS. COBBLER: Mrs. Eunice Cobbler. I live in the large shoe at the end of the block.

ZELLA: Oh, yes, I've noticed it several times. Very unusual. Pointed toes are really in this season.

MRS. COBBLER: Thank you. Anyway, I have all of these children—so many of them, I've totally lost count.

SCOOP: Is that so?

MRS. COBBLER: That's why I'm not sure if I'm missing any. There's Harry and Larry and Mary and Jerry and Terry and Barry and Gary and Perry and Carrie and—

SCOOP: Excuse me, but — (MRS. COBBLER *takes audible deep breath and continues, counting with fingers.*)

MRS. COBBLER: Teddy and Freddie and Nettie and Betty and Cal and Sal and Val and Al—

ZELLA: That's a lot of children!

MRS. COBBLER: You're telling me! It's impossible to keep track of them.

SCOOP: I can see why. Have you considered making a list?

MRS. COBBLER (*Snapping fingers*): Bless my soul! I never thought of that!

ZELLA: You might also want to have them fingerprinted. The police department has a program that makes it easier to keep children safe and sound, whether you have one or a dozen.

MRS. COBBLER: How can I ever thank you?

SCOOP: Forget it. This advice is on the house.

MRS. COBBLER: Oh, thank you so much! (MRS. COBBLER *exits.*)

MRS. PIPER (*Entering*): Pardon me, but do I need an appointment?

ZELLA: Not at all. Come on in.

MRS. PIPER (*Sitting*): I'm Mrs. Piper.

SCOOP: Is your husband Peter Piper?

MRS. PIPER (*Surprised*): Why, yes! Have you heard of him?

SCOOP: He made all the papers last week. Remember, Zella?

ZELLA: Oh, yes, the man who picked some peppers?

SCOOP: Pickled peppers, weren't they?

MRS. PIPER: A peck of them, to be precise.

ZELLA: What's your problem, Mrs. Piper?

MRS. PIPER: Peter seems to have disappeared.

ZELLA: Maybe all the publicity was too much for him.

MRS. PIPER: Possibly. Peter's a pretty private person.

SCOOP: We'll make finding him our priority, Mrs. Piper. I promise.

ZELLA: By the way, where's the peck of pickled peppers Peter Piper picked?

MRS. PIPER: Come to think of it, that's missing too.

SCOOP (*Puzzled*): This case sounds very confusing.

ZELLA: Wait a minute. Do you think Peter took his peppers to the county fair? That would be a perfect place to present his peppers to the public.

MRS. PIPER: I never thought of the fair! Of course! I'll go there on my way home. (*Exits*)

SCOOP (*To* ZELLA; *in admiration*): You're absolutely amazing.

ZELLA (*Shrugging*): All in a day's work.

SCOOP: No, I mean it, Zella. Your ideas are fantastic. What would I do without you?

ZELLA: Well, as the duck said when he didn't have enough cash, "Just put it on my bill." (*Takes files to cabinet*)

SCOOP: Humor aside, Zella, you're efficient, organized, perceptive, talented—I guess I just realized how lost I'd be without you!

ZELLA (*Checking her watch*): Better not miss your next appointment.

SCOOP: Gosh—am I supposed to be somewhere?

ZELLA (*Helping him on with his coat*): At the docks, remember? Captain Hanover's beautiful pea green boat was stolen last night.

SCOOP: Any suspects?

ZELLA: The crew said they've seen a suspicious-looking owl and a pussycat hanging around the marina.

SCOOP (*Helping her on with her coat*): Did they get anything besides the boat?

ZELLA: They took some honey and plenty of money wrapped up in a five-pound note.

SCOOP (*As they walk toward door*): You'd better notify the Coast Guard.

ZELLA: I took care of it as soon as the call came in.

SCOOP (*Smiling*): You're terrific, Zella. I think I've lost my heart!

ZELLA: Good news. (*Straightens his lapels*) I just found it. (*Gives him quick hug, exits; he smiles broadly, puts on his hat and follows her out. Curtain*)

THE END

PRODUCTION NOTES

MOTHER GOOSE GUMSHOE

Characters: 4 female; 1 male.

Playing Time: 10 minutes.

Costumes: Modern dress. Scoop and Zella wear trench coats and hats.

Properties: Purse containing photograph.

Setting: Scoop's office. Desk is center—it has a phone, bulging file folders, telephone books, maps of the city, etc. Chairs for clients are up right of the desk. File cabinets are left. Scoop's trench coat and hat are on coat tree, up right, and exit is right.

Lighting: No special effects.

A Christmas play. . .

It's an Okie-Dokie Life

Characters

HILDEGARDE, *Angel First Class*
SUSANNAH, *Angel Trainee*
JOE, *the depressed hero*
BETSY ⎫ *Joe's little sisters*
MITZI ⎭
LITTLE JOE, *Joe as a kid*
MARY LOU, *Joe's girlfriend*
OLIVER PARSNIP III, *the villain*
TOWNSPEOPLE, *extras*

TIME: *Christmas Eve, the Old West.*
SETTING: *Heaven, Inc., with chair and desk with a computer terminal down left. Played before curtain.*
BEFORE RISE: HILDEGARDE, *wearing starched white gown and enormous wings, is working on computer.* SU-SANNAH, *wearing somewhat dingy gown, stands behind her. Christmas music is heard.*
SUSANNAH (*Gushing*): Oh, I just love Christmas, don't you, Hildegarde? The music, the presents, the cookies . . .
HILDEGARDE (*As she types*): The traffic, the snowstorms, the crowds.
SUSANNAH: Don't be so pessimistic—it's wonderful! (*Giggles*) And you know what's even more wonderful, Hilde-

garde? (*With pride*) This is the year I'm going to do it. I'm going to earn my wings.

HILDEGARDE (*Dismissively*): Oh, Susannah, you've been saying that for the last 420 years.

SUSANNAH: But this time I mean it! I'm going to get my wings and I'll be in Seventh Heaven. (*Scowls*) Or is it Cloud 9? Which is better, Hildegarde?

HILDEGARDE: Well, it depends on—(*Harsh beeping sound suddenly comes from computer*) Uh-oh. (*Types frantically*)

SUSANNAH: What is it?

HILDEGARDE: Red alert. We have a problem down on Earth.

SUSANNAH: What kind?

HILDEGARDE (*Upset*): The worst. (*Shakes head*) And on Christmas Eve, of all nights. (*Types some more*) Oh, no!

SUSANNAH (*Urgently*): What's wrong?

HILDEGARDE: All our best angels are out in the field. It looks like we're going to lose this one.

SUSANNAH (*Excitedly*): Why not let me go?

HILDEGARDE: No, this one's over your head. The boss would never allow it.

SUSANNAH: But if it's a lost cause anyway, what would it matter? Please, Hildegarde! Let me go!

HILDEGARDE (*Thinking it over*): Well . . .

SUSANNAH (*Earnestly*): Please, please! I promise I'll never ask again.

HILDEGARDE (*With a sigh*): O.K. Since there's no one else. (SUSANNAH *starts to run off.*) Wait a minute! Come back here. (SUSANNAH *stops.*) You have to have a briefing first.

SUSANNAH: Right. I almost forgot. (*As they talk, curtain opens. Center is a large bridge with trees and snow banks on either side.*)

HILDEGARDE: Now, pay attention, Susannah. This is very

important. (*From right, a very tired and depressed* JOE
enters.)

SUSANNAH: Who's that?

HILDEGARDE: That, Susannah, is your problem. His
name's Joe. Joe Dakota.

SUSANNAH: He looks sad. (JOE *looks around, starts to
walk up on bridge.*)

HILDEGARDE: Oh, he's worse than sad tonight, Susannah.
You see, this afternoon Joe lost the payroll for the ranch.
A lot of people are going to go without Christmas dinner
because he can't pay them.

SUSANNAH: So he's looking for the money in the snow? Is
that what I have to help him with?

HILDEGARDE: No, it's much more serious than that. You'll
have to help Joe find himself.

SUSANNAH: That's easy. He's right there.

HILDEGARDE: But not for long. In less than sixty seconds,
Joe is going to make a terrible mistake . . . unless someone
is there to stop him. Someone like you, Susannah.

SUSANNAH (*In panic*): But what do I do? What do I say?

HILDEGARDE: That's part of your test as an angel, Susannah. It's up to you. (*Looks at her watch*) Forty-five seconds.
(SUSANNAH *runs off left*) Oh, I do hope I've done the
right thing. She's wanted her wings for so long! (*More
cheerfully*) Maybe this is just the kind of assignment she's
been waiting for. For Joe's sake, I hope so. (*As the lights
dim on* HILDEGARDE, SUSANNAH *rushes on left. She
now wears jeans, boots and a plaid shirt.* JOE *is leaning
over the side of the bridge.*)

SUSANNAH (*Shouting*): Hey there! (*Rushes up to him*)

JOE (*Startled*): Whoa! You got a mean holler there, little
lady. A fellow could fall in.

SUSANNAH: Yes, I know. (*Looks down*) Pretty deep, isn't
it?

JOE (*Shrugging*): Deep enough. (*Notices her*) Say, you shouldn't be out in this kind of weather in your shirt sleeves. (*Takes off jacket*) Here you go, miss.

SUSANNAH: That's really kind of you, Joe.

JOE (*Puzzled*): Have we met before?

SUSANNAH: Not exactly.

JOE: Then how did you know my name?

SUSANNAH: Well—promise not to laugh?

JOE: Sure.

SUSANNAH: I'm a guardian angel. (JOE *laughs.*) You promised not to laugh.

JOE: A guardian angel, huh? So where are your wings?

SUSANNAH (*Uncomfortably*): Well, I don't have them yet. You see, first I have to do a good deed. And when I do, they'll play Beethoven's Ninth Symphony, and ta-da! I'll finally be an official angel.

JOE: Yeah, well, I sure could use one, miss—uh, what's your name?

SUSANNAH: Susannah. And that's why I'm here. To help you.

JOE: Nobody can help me, Miss Susannah. I let a lot of people down tonight. They'd be better off if I'd never been around in the first place.

SUSANNAH (*Firmly*): But that's not true, Joe!

JOE: Yes, it is. That's why I came here tonight. (*Smiles*) You can keep the jacket. (*Starts to climb over*)

SUSANNAH (*Grabbing him*): Wait!

JOE: Wait for what?

SUSANNAH (*Thinking fast*): What if I could give you your wish?

JOE: What wish?

SUSANNAH: To see what it would be like without you?

JOE (*Surprised*): Can you do that?

SUSANNAH (*Worriedly*): I don't know. I've never tried. (*With enthusiasm*) But it's worth a shot, don't you think?

JOE (*Shrugging*): Sure, I suppose. What do I do?

SUSANNAH: Just watch. (*Waves her arms wildly and makes up a chant*)

Flutter, butter, flutter-fly,

Swiftly let the years go by!

Crystal whistle busy-buzz,

Show us now what wasn't was.

(BETSY *and* MITZI, *giggling, enter left.*)

SUSANNAH (*Delighted*): Oh, my goodness! It really worked!

JOE: Betsy! Mitzi!

SUSANNAH: Do you know them?

JOE: Sure—they're my kid sisters. (*Calls*) Hey, Betsy! Mitzi!

SUSANNAH: They can't hear you, Joe. We're looking at the past. Your past.

LITTLE JOE (*Entering from right*): Hey, you two!

JOE: Why, that's me when I was a kid!

LITTLE JOE: You gals better be careful! There's an old quicksand trap out in these parts.

BETSY: We'll be careful!

MITZI: We always are!

LITTLE JOE: All the same, I think you'd better come home.

BETSY: Oh, come on, Joe!

MITZI: Yeah, we're just having fun!

BETSY: Come on, Mitzi, let's play tag.

MITZI: O.K. (*Girls starts to run as* LITTLE JOE *walks downstage. Suddenly, they mime falling into quicksand.*)

BETSY: Help!

MITZI: Help! Quicksand! (LITTLE JOE *runs off.*)

JOE (*To* SUSANNAH): Hey! Where am I going?

SUSANNAH: Don't you remember, Joe? You ran off to get some rope. (LITTLE JOE *runs back on with rope, which he tosses to* BETSY *and* MITZI.)

LITTLE JOE: Grab hold and don't let go!

SUSANNAH: Without thinking of danger to yourself, you risked your life that day to save Betsy and Mitzi from a horrible fate. (LITTLE JOE, *after much struggle, pulls girls from quicksand.*)

BETSY *and* MITZI (*Ad lib as they hug him*): You saved our lives, Joe! What would we have done without you? (*Etc.* BETSY, MITZI, *and* LITTLE JOE *exit.*)

SUSANNAH: If it hadn't been for your quick thinking, Joe, Betsy wouldn't be the mayor of Tombstone today, and Mitzi wouldn't be a best-selling novelist.

JOE: Aw—that was just luck. Anybody could have done it. (*He sits on bridge, his back to the audience.*)

SUSANNAH (*Looking upward as lights dim on bridge scene*): It isn't working, Hildegarde! (*Spotlight comes up on* HILDEGARDE.) He isn't listening.

HILDEGARDE: Don't give up, Susannah. You're Joe's last chance tonight. You've got to show him that people really care. (*During this partial blackout,* JOE *exits, and another actor dressed in same clothes takes* JOE's *place on the bridge. He keeps his back to audience. The light goes out on* HILDEGARDE, *comes up on* SUSANNAH *again.*)

SUSANNAH: Joe, so many people really do care about you. In fact, the one who cares the most is worried to death right now. Do you remember how you met Mary Lou, Joe? It was at this very river, when you were just a kid out fishing. (*Giggles*) She caught a fish bigger than yours, too. I think you knew even then that she was your kind of girl. And remember the day you proposed? (MARY LOU *strolls on right.*)

JOE (*Running on*): Mary Lou! Wait up!

MARY LOU (*With shy smile*): Hi, Joe.

JOE: Mary Lou, I have to ask you something.

MARY LOU: Yes?

JOE (*Pacing nervously*): I've been giving it a lot of thought. About us, I mean. About how right we are for each other.

MARY LOU (*Shyly*): What are you saying, Joe?

JOE (*Blurting it out, as he takes her hand*): Mary Lou, I've got two thousand dollars and five in loose change. I figure it's enough to put down on a little ranch, buy some livestock, and—

MARY LOU: And?

JOE: Would you share it with me, Mary Lou? Be my wife?

MARY LOU: Oh, Joe! (*Hugs him*)

JOE: Does that mean yes? (*She laughs.*)

MARY LOU: I've been waiting for this day—(*A shout from right interrupts their happy scene, as* TOWNSPEOPLE *enter carrying suitcases and looking sad.*)

1ST TOWNSPERSON: Hey, Joe!

JOE: Hey, Leroy! (*Acknowledges others*) Ethel May, Barney, Muriel—(*Scratches his head*) You folks all taking off on a vacation?

2ND TOWNSPERSON: We're leaving town, Joe. We came to say goodbye.

JOE (*Incredulous*): Leaving town?

MARY LOU: But this is your home!

3RD TOWNSPERSON (*Shaking his head*): Not any more.

4TH TOWNSPERSON: He's running us out.

JOE (*Puzzled*): Who?

1ST TOWNSPERSON: Who else? Oliver Parsnip III.

5TH TOWNSPERSON: The banker. He's foreclosing on all our farms, Joe.

6TH TOWNSPERSON: He said the mortgage was due by sundown. We couldn't pay him.

JOE: How much did he want? (OLIVER PARSNIP III, *looking villainous, enters left. All turn when he speaks.*)

PARSNIP (*Authoritatively*): They have to pay me two thousand dollars! (*Laughs evilly*) A little out of their range, I'd say.

MARY LOU (*Angrily*): How can you be so cruel? These people have lived here all their lives!

JOE: You own half the town already, Parsnip.

PARSNIP: Yes, and I'd like to own the other half, as well—(*Looks at pocketwatch*)—which I will in precisely three minutes.

1ST TOWNSPERSON (*Sadly*): Take care of yourself, Joe. (TOWNSPEOPLE *start to exit.*)

JOE (*Stopping them*): Hold on! None of you has to leave if you don't want to.

PARSNIP (*Harshly*): And how do you plan to stop it?

JOE (*Reaching inside shirt and dramatically withdrawing money*): With this. (*Striding up to* PARSNIP) There's two thousand dollars, Parsnip. (*Slapping it into* PARSNIP'*s hand*) Their debt to you is paid. Now, get on out of here! (PARSNIP *sneers and skulks off as the crowd cheers and ad libs their gratitude to* JOE.)

2ND TOWNSPERSON: I can't believe you did that, Joe!

3RD TOWNSPERSON: Joe's our hero!

MARY LOU: Oh, Joe, you're wonderful!

JOE (*With a sigh*): I had to do it. There's just one problem. Now I've got only five dollars to my name, Mary Lou.

MARY LOU (*Warmly*): I wouldn't care if it was five cents. My answer is still "yes." I'll marry you. (MARY LOU *and* JOE *exit right.* TOWNSPEOPLE *in front of bridge provide substantial cover for* JOE *to take his stand-in's place on bridge.*)

4TH TOWNSPERSON: Thanks to Joe, we still have our land!

1ST TOWNSPERSON: We owe Joe a lot. He sure showed that Parsnip a thing or two.

3RD TOWNSPERSON: Parsnip will never push us around again!

6TH TOWNSPERSON (*As they exit*): Joe is a great guy!

SUSANNAH: A lot of people wouldn't still be in this town if it weren't for you, Joe.

JOE (*Stretching as he stands*): Yeah, I suppose.

SUSANNAH: And remember how humiliated Mr. Parsnip was?

JOE (*Chuckling*): Yep. Moved out of town that night and hasn't been heard from since.

SUSANNAH: And remember how you saved all those books in the library fire?

JOE (*Nodding*): I'd almost forgotten about that.

SUSANNAH: And how about all those people you gave jobs to when you first got your ranch going?

JOE (*Despairingly*): Oh, no.

SUSANNAH: What's wrong?

JOE: The ranch. The payroll. I'd almost forgotten that, too. You've cheered me up.

SUSANNAH (*Softly*): Your workers will understand, Joe.

JOE: But it's Christmas Eve. I can't go back there empty-handed.

SUSANNAH: Maybe you can. (*Seriously*) Your friends know you are always generous—every day, not just at Christmas time. Every life touches another, Joe, no matter how small it may seem.

JOE: Yeah, I guess you're right.

SUSANNAH: Go back and explain. They'll understand. Oh— and here's your jacket. (*Takes jacket off and hands it to him*) Thanks for letting me borrow it.

JOE: Well, where are you going? (*Before she can answer, the swell of Beethoven's Ninth Symphony is heard. SUSANNAH squeals. JOE looks puzzled.*) What's that music?

SUSANNAH (*Excitedly*): I did it, Joe! At least I think I did! They always play Beethoven's Ninth when an angel gets her wings. I'd better get back and see if I'm the one this time. (*Starts to run off*)

JOE: Hey, Susannah?

SUSANNAH (*Stopping to look back*): Yes?

JOE: Good luck! And thanks! (*She exits as* MARY LOU *and* TOWNSPEOPLE *enter right.*)

4TH TOWNSPERSON: There he is!

MARY LOU: Joe! Joe! (*Embraces him*) We've been looking all over for you.

2ND TOWNSPERSON: Mary Lou found your note, Joe.

1ST TOWNSPERSON: The one about the payroll.

3RD TOWNSPERSON: We tried to find it for you.

JOE (*Eagerly*): Did you? Have you got it with you?

MARY LOU: No. It's really lost, Joe.

6TH TOWNSPERSON: But don't forget the good news, Mary Lou.

JOE: What good news?

2ND TOWNSPERSON (*Stepping forward*): We all got together and took up a collection. (*Hands* JOE *a sack*) This should cover the payroll just fine.

JOE (*Touched*): I don't know how I can think you enough. It may take me awhile, but I'll pay all of you back for this, every cent.

3RD TOWNSPERSON: It shouldn't take that long, Joe.

JOE (*Puzzled*): What do you mean?

6TH TOWNSPERSON (*Smiling*): That's the rest of the good news.

1ST TOWNSPERSON: You've got a geyser of oil right on your land, Joe. It's shooting up higher than Old Faithful!

JOE: Oil? (*Tosses hat in air*) Yahoo! (TOWNSPEOPLE *cheer and exit as* JOE *hugs* MARY LOU.)

MARY LOU: Brr, it's cold. (*He gives her his jacket.*) What are you doing out here anyway, Joe?

JOE: Oh, just thinking that it's an okie-dokie life . . . (*Sound of Beethoven's Ninth is heard.*)

MARY LOU: What was that?

JOE (*Smiling*): I think an angel just got her wings. (*Hugs* MARY LOU. *Down left, at Heaven, Inc., lights come up as* SUSANNAH *enters in starched white gown and huge wings.*)

HILDEGARDE (*Beaming*): You did it, Susannah. You really did it.

SUSANNAH (*Winking*): Did you ever have any doubts? (*They both look over at* JOE *and* SUSANNAH.)

JOE: Let's go home, honey.

SUSANNAH: Merry Christmas, Joe. (JOE *and* MARY LOU *walk off.* JOE *stops a moment and looks up, listening, as if he'd heard* SUSANNAH.)

MARY LOU: What is it?

JOE: Oh, nothing. I'm just feeling Christmas in the air. (*Urges* MARY LOU *to go ahead of him, which she does.* JOE *looks in direction of Heaven, Inc., and mouths* "*Merry Christmas.*" *Curtain*)

THE END

Production Notes

IT'S AN OKIE-DOKIE LIFE

Characters: 5 female, 3 male; extras for Townspeople and Joe's stand-in.

Playing Time: 15 minutes.

Costumes: Joe and his stand-in wear identical jeans, boots, shirt and Stetson. Joe wears jacket. Old West attire for Betsy, Mitzi, Little Joe, Mary Lou, and for Susannah on earth. Susannah wears dingy gown in Heaven, Inc., before she gets wings. Hildegarde wears starched white gown with wings, as does Susannah at end of play. Parsnip wears black sinister clothes, and carries pocket watch.

Properties: Rope, suitcases, money, sack.

Setting: Heaven, Inc., with chair and desk with computer terminal down left. Played before curtain. Behind curtain and center is large bridge with trees and snow banks on either side.

Lighting: Dimming and spotlight, as indicated.

Sound: Computer beeping, Beethoven's Ninth Symphony, Christmas music.